East Side Story

* --- *

PEOPLE AND PLACES IN THE

HISTORY OF EAST TOLEDO

* --- * --- * --- *

Larry R. Michaels

Bihl House Publishing
Toledo, Ohio
1993

The author gratefully acknowleges the encouragement of Scott Carpenter of THE PRESS NEWSPAPERS, which includes the METRO, SUBURBAN, and PRIMETIME, and also of Lee Raizk and BEND OF THE RIVER MAGAZINE. Many sections of this book first appeared in these publications.

Published September 1st in an edition of 200 hard cover and 800 soft cover copies. Fifty hard cover copies have been numbered and signed. Printed and bound by Edwards Brothers, Ann Arbor, MI

2nd printing, December 1993
3rd printing, October 1994
4th printing, June 1996
5th printing, May 1999
6th printing, January 2003

ISBN 1-883829-11-9

ISBN 1-883829-12-7 (pbk)

This book is dedicated

to

~ JEFF EVERSMAN

and in memory of

CAL O. GETTINGS

CONTENTS

1878

View from the East Side in 1866.

INTRODUCTION

EAST TOLEDO HISTORY: AN OVERVIEW

Peter Navarre and his brothers, who were French-Canadian fur trappers, first settled east of the Maumee River about 1807. Five years later when the War of 1812 broke out, Peter and Robert served as scouts for General William Henry Harrison, who was commander of the garrison at Fort Meigs.

During the fighting of 1813, Peter Navarre carried important messages from General Harrison to Commodore Perry and to Major George Croghan. He was also involved in the Battle of the Thames River in Ontario where Chief Tecumseh was killed and the British were finally forced to retreat from the Great Lakes region.

Even after the war was over, because of the difficulty in crossing the Great Black Swamp, settlers were slow to arrive in what is now East Toledo. Virgin forests covered much of the area, along with the swales that still can be traced from the depressions of old creek beds weaving their way through the East Side. Swales, or "hollows," were marshy depressions that after spring rains provided breeding grounds for the insects that brought debilitating diseases like malaria, or "the ague."

Pioneers

Not long after the War of 1812, however, some rugged pioneers began to brave the wilderness. The Prentice, Whitmore, and Crane families owned land east of the river by the 1820's. According to

Isaac Wright's history of the East Side (1894), Isaac
Worden built the first house along the river bank
near Oak Street in 1826, the same year he and John
Baldwin broke the first ground, three acres for
corn. By 1830, the Potter farm and the Bissell and
Hicks farms were established.

Also in the 1830s, a cluster of buildings
sprang up near what is now Miami Street and Oregon
Road, one of several hopeful "towns" along the river
that were destined to fail. A Quaker named Isaac
Street, who developed this first "Oregon," was sold
out at auction when it was learned that the canal
would be located on the other side of the river.

Mr. Street had the last word, however,
because the name he chose survived as the name of
the township for the whole area east of the Maumee
River. The first election in Oregon Township took
place on July 4th, 1837, and Joseph Prentice, Hiram
Brown, and Isaac Street were elected judges.

During the 1830s and 1840s several other
settlers arrived, including Elijah Woodruff, Asa
Maddocks, Louis Metzger, J. C. Messer, Romeyn
Rogers, Mary Berry, Aaron Ryno, Ezra Howland,
Oliver Stevens, John Consaul, John Fassett, Richard
Eggleston, Nathan Gardner, and many others. The
first business on the East Side was Thomas
Bradberry's saw mill in 1848, and the first store was
opened by Victor Plumey the following year.

"Utah" and the Civil War

In 1851, Judge Potter, who represented
Oregon Township in Congress, brought the first Post
Office to the East Side. He called it "Utah" because
he thought the people liked western names. Elijah
Woodruff was the first postmaster, followed by James
Raymer.

The only roads on the East Side were the Woodville plank road and the River Road. In 1853, Oak Street was surveyed and Cherry Street (now Euclid) was laid out. Also during the 1850s the first regular plats of housing lots were planned. Main Street (at first called Bridge Street) was not opened until 1873.

Travel was difficult in those early days, but that did not deter the hardy settlers in the outlying areas of Oregon Township. The Bay Shore area was given to the Navarre family for their services during the War of 1812, and the Indians were forced to leave during the late 1830s. Some of the other pioneer families who settled on the rich farmland east of the river were the Momanys, Mominees, Coys, Millers, Rideouts, Messers, Browns, and many other familiar names still living in Oregon today.

In 1854, the East Side suffered a severe cholera epidemic. At that time there were about 175 people living in Utah, and over one third of them perished, including Victor Plumey and his wife Clarissa, Ambrose Rogers, Daniel Coy, and Francis Momany along with his wife and six children. About thirty of the victims were buried under an apple tree near the corner of Starr and Oak, even then a popular playground for children from the old wooden school near Oak and Front. The first Franklin School was built on land adjacent to the cemetery just seventeen years later.

The Yondota plat of Oregon Township became part of Toledo in 1853. The city decided to incorporate the East Side primarily because the railroads ended east of the then bridgeless river.

Many East Siders fought in the Civil War. In 1862, there were 116 men from the Sixth Ward who voted in the election for Congress that year. Of those adult men, 61 would fight in the war and eleven lose their lives. Captain George Scheets of

the Ford Post has preserved a record of all East
Side veterans in a history still accessible at the
Main Library in downtown Toledo. A famous veteran
named Wilson Brown, who received one of the first
Congressional Medals of Honor as a member of the
daring Andrews Raiders, spent his last years in East
Toledo.

Boom Years of Rapid Growth

Not until after the Civil War was the first
bridge constructed across the Maumee River, and for
several more years it charged an unpopular toll.
But when a sturdier, free bridge was opened during
the 1870s, the East Side began to grow rapidly. An
estimated population of only 500 in 1861 had grown
to 5,000 by 1884. Eight years later that number had
more than doubled to 12,000. By the turn of the
century there were nearly 18,000 inhabitants in East
Toledo, by 1910 there were 27,198, and by 1930 over
46,000. Today, two-thirds of that number live within
the present boundaries of East Toledo.

The years between the early 1880s and the
1920s were the boom years for East Toledo. During
that time oil was discovered, and soon the East Side
became an important oil refining and shipping
center. Ship-building prospered along the river.
More railroads were built. Streetcar lines and the
automobile connected East Siders more closely with
the rest of the city. The Fassett Street Bridge
opened in 1895, and the Ash-Consaul not long
afterwards.

Bridge Street, renamed Main Street in 1894,
replaced the area at Front and Euclid as the favorite
East Side business address. Anchoring the corner
of Front and Main were the old Plumey Block (1874)
which later became the Garbe Block and is now
Wendy's, the Platt Building (1886) which is now
McDonald's, and the Weber Block (1888).

The prosperous 1890s saw the building of the Friedman Block (later a Penney's store) and the Montville Block (home of Barrett's Shoe Store) at First and Main, the Arlington Hotel at Second Street, and the Coad Building and Davies Block at Sixth and Main. All but the Montville and Arlington are still standing. E. J. Smith's opened on Starr Avenue during the 1890's, and Engine House #6 was built at Starr and Main in 1895. Some of the other best remembered businesses included Metzger's, Flory's, Save's, Redd's, Reddish's, Ringenbach's, Popoff's, VonEwegen's, Lownsbury's, and many more.

Industries and Ethnic Neighborhoods

The East Side's industrial boom years also added to its rich ethnic heritage. The Navarres were French-Canadian, and later a prominent French community settled in the East Broadway and Greenwood (originally called French Street) area. Many immigrants from Alsace-Lorraine, the region between Germany and France, came to the East Side bringing names like Gladieux, Bihl, Bihn, Plumey, Metzger, and Hollerbach.

As early as the 1860s there was an Iron mill that led to settlement and finally gave its name to the Ironville area. Then in the early 1890s the National Malleable Castings Company located on Front Street near Consaul, providing jobs for the hundreds of Hungarian immigrants who came seeking work and then settled nearby. Families named Orosz, Bertok, Paczko (Packo), Nagy, Kertesz, and many others have maintained Birmingham's strong Hungarian heritage.

Industries also led to the development of other areas in East Toledo. The large rolling mill that stood where the Edison Acme plant is today brought people to live in the Mott Avenue district. The growth of the Sun Oil Company led people to

build homes out Woodville Road, and the old pump
works and linseed oil mills brought people to the
East Broadway-Oakdale area. "Cottonwood"
developed from the railroads and the Smith Bridge
Company in that area. And of course Rossford,
which was built up around Captain Ford's Plate
Glass Company at the turn of the century, took its
name from Mr. Ford and his wife, Caroline Ross.

Among other ethnic groups that settled the
East Side were the Bulgarians. Located primarily
around the Front and Main area, they ran many
popular businesses and restaurants, and built a
Bulgarian-Macedonian Church close by on Oswald
Street. In addition, Italian and Greek and Hispanic
and African-American families have all found homes
over the years in East Toledo.

Schools, Churches, and Parks

Schools have always played an important role
in the development of the East Side. The first log
school was built along the river near the foot of
what is now Consaul Street in 1837, and two years
later classes were being held in a board shanty at
Front and Euclid. Mrs. Mary Berry was the first
teacher in both schools, and Mrs. Sarah Denman also
taught on the East Side during the 1840s.

For several years, other small frame school-
houses were built in the Front and Oak Street area,
until the first brick Franklin School was constructed
in 1871 at Fourth and Steadman. Even though two
large additions were added during the 1880s and
90s, by 1924 it was necessary to build a new
Franklin School at the same site.

By the time East Toledo's population peaked in
the early 1930s, Oakdale and Garfield schools had
been built, and the old Navarre, Birmingham,
Raymer, and Franklin schools had been replaced

with newer structures. East Side Central was built
in 1895, and until Waite opened in 1913-14, it served
as the first three years of high school for East Side
students. A new East Side Central was constructed
in 1960.

During the second half of the nineteenth
century, many one-room schools were built in
Oregon and Jerusalem townships. Brandville School,
built in 1882, still stands on Grasser Street near
Pickle Road and today is the home of the Oregon-
Jerusalem Historical Society.

Several parochial schools have also served the
East Side over the years. Sacred Heart School at
Sixth and Morrison was built in 1889, remodeled in
1954, and is still going strong. Good Shepherd
School closed recently after well over a century of
educating East Toledo children. St. Stephen's
Parish in Birmingham and St. Thomas Aquinas on
Idaho Street both have large elementary schools.

Waite High School has remained a centerpiece
for the East Side community for over 75 years.
When Waite and Scott were the only high schools in
Toledo, students came to the East Side from as far
away as Tribly. Known for its athletic programs,
Waite won eighteen city championships in football
between 1921 and 1963.

The East Side is also known for its beautiful
churches. Sacred Heart, Good Shepherd, St. Louis,
St. Stephen's, and St. Thomas are Catholic Parishes
all within the boundaries of East Toledo. Among
Protestant congregations, St. Mark, Martin Luther,
Euclid Avenue Methodist, Second Baptist, Calvin
United Church of Christ, and several others have
landmark East Side buildings.

Some of Toledo's earliest parks are also on the
East Side. Prentice Park, the old "Flat-iron Park"
was donated to the city as a Village Green in 1858,

making it Toledo's oldest park. During the 1890s,
Oliver Stevens donated the land that became Navarre
Park and Judge Collins also gave land for a park
that bears his name. Pearson Park, the old railroad
"Bank Lands", was saved for a park through the
efforts of Blade columnist George Pearson, and is
one of the most used Metroparks today.

*   *   *

Much history has happened east of the
Maumee during the 186 years since the Navarres
settled out on the Bay Shore. But since Isaac
Wright published The East Side in 1894, no history
of East Toledo has been attempted. Although a
detailed history of all our churches, schools,
businesses, and important houses must await future
publications, the chapters that follow were written
to preserve and highlight some of those people,
places, and events that have played a significant
role in our East Side Story.

East Toledo in 1876.

Chapter 1

IN THE BEGINNING...

*

The East Side

from

The Wilderness

to

The War of 1812

*

HISTORIC MARKER ALL THAT REMAINS OF INDIAN FORT

Today there is only the continuous flow of trucks at the grain elevators on Miami Street just south of Fassett. Miami Street is four lanes wide at that point, and few motorists have time to notice the four-ton sandstone marker with a bronze tablet that stands beside the road. Fort Meigs has been restored and Fort Miamis excavated, but that marker, dwarfed by the huge grain elevators, is all that remains of the East Side's prehistoric Indian fort.

The age of the fort is uncertain. Judge J. H. Doyle, who wrote a history of early Toledo, described the mounds as the "most pretentious" of the four Indian earthworks found in the area. The fort was also the only local Indian remains surveyed by Squire and Davis for the Smithsonian when they made their inspection of prehistoric mounds in 1848. Their report showed that the fort was as large as three acres.

Another early witness, Charles Whittlesey, wrote that the fort sat on a bluff that was about 35 feet above the river at that time, and the dirt mounds were three to four feet high. Ditches were dug around the base of the mounds, and in places there was a double wall. A few skeletons were found in the mounds, according to Whittlesey, but they were thought to be later Indian burials. It seems that the earthworks were definitely constructed for defensive purposes.

The marker commemorating this important East Side landmark was dedicated a month before Pearl Harbor in November of 1941, by the Fort Industry Chapter of the Daughters of the American Revolution. Several other organizations in that part of East Toledo were also involved, including Hathaway School, Memorial Baptist and Clark Street Methodist Churches, East Side Hospital on Oak Street, and the Railroad YMCA that stood at the corner of Oak and Fassett. Because of inclement weather, the ceremonies were held at Clark Street Methodist, except for the actual unveiling.

The number of prominent people involved in the dedication attests to the importance East Siders of that time placed on keeping the memory of the fort alive. Harlow Lindley of the Ohio Historical Association was there, as was E. C. Zepp, curator of the Ohio State Museum, who wrote the inscription for the marker. Also in attendance were Gardner Williams of The University of Toledo, Max Shepherst

of the Metropolitan Park Board, and Mrs. Shepherst
from the library's local history department. George
Pearson gave a history of the fort, and Mrs. Mark
Winchester unveiled the marker.

Dedication of Indian Fort Marker, 1941.

The inscription on the monument describes
and illustrates the earthworks and moats, and
speculates that the mounds were topped with
"palisades" which made the fort fairly secure from
attack. Some believe that the fort was built by the
Erie Nation of Indians who lived in the area prior to
1655. The location at the bend in the river gave the
defenders an unobstructed view in both directions
and prevented a "surprise attack from enemy
canoemen."

Today that view is blocked by the grain

elevators. Even the name of Fort Street, which kept
the memory alive for many years, has been changed
to Hathaway Street. Now all that remains of the fort
is a four-ton marker and its recently restored
bronze inscription. Maybe Mrs. Breitenwischer said
it best in her dedication speech that day in 1941:
"Nothing is really ended until it is forgotten.
Whatever is kept in memory still endures."

TECUMSEH AND THE WAR OF 1812

On March 9, 1768, a great meteor flashed
across the sky from north to south and left a fiery
trail that could be seen by all Native Americans
living east of the Mississippi. Indian lore
interpreted this as a sign from the heavens
heralding a momentous event. The day the meteor
appeared a child was born in the family of
Puckenshinwa, second-in-command of all Shawnee
warriors.

The child was named Tecumseh, which meant
"The Panther Passing Across," because of the meteor
passing across the sky. Puckenshinwa was killed
when the boy was only six. From his older brother,
however, Tecumseh learned bravery in battle, and
from a sister he learned to reject cruelty and to
have compassion for the weak and helpless.

In early skirmishes with white settlers in
Ohio, Tecumseh quickly became known for his
courage and leadership. Word of "a new demon
chief" spread among the settlements. He was not
only fearless, but also handsome, muscular, and tall.
One American soldier described him as "one of the
most dignified men I ever beheld."

Tecumseh's dream was to unite the tribes

north of the Ohio River to prevent the white man from pushing them off their native lands. Through his younger brother, known as the Prophet, Tecumseh tried to show other Indians he was acting on behalf of the Great Spirit. Once when General Harrison challenged the Prophet to produce a sign that he could predict the future, Tecumseh, who had learned from the British of a total eclipse of the sun, shrewdly told his brother to predict the sun would blacken on that day. Warriors from the other tribes were convinced of the Prophet's powers when the sun did indeed disappear for seven minutes, only to be called back by the chants of the Prophet.

Unfortunately for Tecumseh, his brother became arrogant and power hungry. In September 1811, when Tecumseh was away visiting southern tribes, the Prophet convinced the Indian warriors to attack General Harrison's strong encampment at Tippecanoe. He had promised them that he could turn the white soldiers' bullets into water. The Indians were badly defeated, making Harrison a military hero, and the braves from a dozen tribes returned home completely disillusioned. Tecumseh was furious, and he began to realize that his dream of an Indian nation would never be fulfilled.

Tecumseh joined forces with the British during the War of 1812 in a final attempt to protect the Indian homelands. Tecumseh worked well with General Isaac Brock, in whom he recognized bravery and leadership to match his own. However, when Brock was killed at Niagara, he was replaced by the ineffective Colonel Henry Proctor, a weak man Tecumseh could not respect.

Proctor callously allowed Indians to massacre wounded American prisoners after the Battle of Frenchtown on the Raisin River near present day Monroe, Michigan. Then when he also permitted the slaughter of 150 prisoners of Dudley's command, Tecumseh himself rode to their rescue. After restraining the Indians, he then called the ashen-faced Proctor a squaw and told him, "Go, put on your petticoats!" In the end, despite Tecumseh's skillful leadership, the American forces overcame the feeble resistance of the British.

As a last resort, Tecumseh persuaded the retreating British armies to make a final stand at the Thames River in Ontario. In the close fighting on October 5, 1813, Tecumseh was shot and killed. With their Chief dead, the Indians melted into the forest, never again to be united under one leader. After the Treaty of Ghent, they pledged themselves to the American side and were gradually shipped to reservations far from their native homelands.

The American victory at Thames River, along with Perry's defeat of the British fleet on Lake Erie a few weeks earlier, opened the way for many more settlers to come into Northwest Ohio. Their only remaining enemy would be the Great Black Swamp.

VICTORIA CADARACT: LAST OF THE CHIPPEWA

When she died on March 23, 1915, Victoria Cadaract was the last of the Chippewa Tribe and probably the last full-blooded Native-American left from the pioneer days in Northwest Ohio. Living in a small, dilapidated cabin near Curtice, on what is now the Chippewa Golf Course, Mrs. Cadaract kept alive the memory of her ancestors who once roamed all the land in this region.

Because she remembered stories of Indian braves preparing to attack Fort Meigs in 1813, she was believed to be 105 years old at the time of her death. The 1900 U.S. Census for Allen Township, Ottawa County, however, records her birth as

February 1828.

She was born in Ohio, as were both of her parents. Her grandfather was chief of the tribe which owned much of the land around Presque Isle and Ironville. He once mocked the British soldiers stationed in the area by dressing in a red uniform and strutting around waving a military sword "much to the delight of the braves about him."

Mrs. Cadaract's father apparently died when she was young, and her mother remarried Francis Navarre, the older brother of Peter and Robert Navarre. Her husband, who was of half French descent, also died young, leaving her a widow for the greater part of her long life. According to the 1880 Census, she had a son Peter (1864) and a daughter Catherine (1866), and her occupation was listed as "basket maker."

Though she remained very independent all her life, Mrs. Cadaract had many friends among the white settlers. Her cabin stood on a large farm owned by Thad Taylor, and he insisted that his workers also plow land for her garden so that she could grow the corn, potatoes, and beans she needed to survive. Mr. Taylor and his wife Harriet, who later owned the house at Starr and Euclid that became the East Side YMCA and Toddler Nursery, were largely responsible, along with Louis Metzger, for preserving the memory of Mrs. Cadaract's life.

She was a proud woman and refused to accept charity. When she was past eighty, and had lost almost the entire sight in one eye, she still walked the two miles into Curtice to buy the few goods she needed. Her neighbors tried to help, however, and in December 1898 a local newspaper reported, "The people of Curticeville held a box social at the church Wednesday night for the benefit of Mrs. Cadaract, an old Indian woman."

Her pride is also apparent in the well-known story of the Navarre Monument. Because of her close connection with the Navarre family, she was invited to the July 4, 1914 dedication of the new monument to Peter and Robert at Navarre Park. She was 86 years old and had less than a year to live, but according to an account at the time, she refused to attend the ceremony because "she had not done her washing yet and could not think of going out unless her wearing apparel was in order."

By this time she was "tired" and had trouble "getting about." In early March 1915, she fell and broke her femur, and thirteen days later she died of pneumonia in the Ottawa County Infirmary at Oak Harbor. The proud Indian woman who in her youth witnessed the forced evacuation of her people from their homelands lies in an unmarked grave in Allen Township Cemetery, a grave she had purchased herself many years before for two dollars.

PETER NAVARRE: FIRST EAST SIDE SETTLER

During the War of 1812, Peter Navarre was the man with the thousand dollar scalp.

Navarre, with his knowledge of the Indians and the northwestern Ohio wilderness, was a valuable scout and source of information for the American military leaders. The British, frustrated by his ability to avoid capture, offered the Indians this huge reward for his life. Peter Navarre's scalp, however, remained firmly in place, and he lived well past his 80th birthday.

Peter Navarre was born in Detroit about 1790, the date of his baptism at St. Ann's Parish, although other sources cite the year 1785. Navarre and his four brothers settled east of the Maumee River in 1807, by all accounts the first permanent American settlers in the area.   Their French-Canadian grandfather, Robert Navarre, visited what is now the East Side as early as 1745 to buy furs from the Indians. The Navarre brothers also traded with the Indians, and Peter became trusted by the Miamis and spoke the Pottawatomi dialect. He was known for his gentlemanly bearing and his skill at wood-working.

The Great Lakes were the crucial battleground between the British and Americans during the War of 1812.   The British with their Indian allies had already defeated the American forces at Detroit and Frenchtown (Monroe). By in 1813, however, General William Henry Harrison, the future President, was in command of the American army located at the newly constructed Fort Meigs, and was able to withstand two separate seiges by the British and the Indians. Also by that time, Admiral Oliver Hazard Perry had arrived at Put-in-Bay to challenge Admiral Barclay's British fleet.

It was at this critical point in the war that Peter Navarre proved so helpful to both Harrison and Perry.   On August 5, 1813, he brought a message from Perry at Port Clinton to General Harrison at Fort Meigs saying that more soldiers were needed.   Consequently, Harrison sent some Kentucky sharpshooters who proved to be very valuable during the battle that would soon follow. Navarre also led them through the wilderness to join Perry's fleet.

Then on September 9th, Navarre is credited with delivering perhaps the most important message of the war. Given little chance to get through the British lines, he disguised himself as an Indian and was able to reach Admiral Perry with General Harrison's plea to engage the enemy as soon as possible.   Perry responded immediately and the famous Battle of Lake Erie was fought the next day.

Most historians agree that it was Navarre who also brought Perry's often-quoted reply back to General Harrison: "We have met the enemy and they are ours."

Navarre himself later recalled another mission as his most difficult. He was asked by General Harrison to make the thirty-mile trip to Fort Stephenson (Fremont) to warn the garrison of a British attack. Navarre would have to travel all night through the Black Swamp in a fierce thunderstorm to reach the fort. Although there is some doubt as to how the warning reached Major Croghan in time, he did indeed know of the British attack and was able to hold the fort against overwhelming odds.

Peter Navarre also fought at the Battle of the Thames River where Tecumseh was killed and the British army was driven out of the Great Lakes region for the final time.

After the war, Navarre remained on the East Side and continued to trade with the friendly Miami Indians. He worked for a fur company based in Detroit, and often traveled to the Fort Wayne area. For his services during the war his family was deeded the "Navarre Tract" of former Indian land out along the Bay Shore, and he lived on that property in a log cabin that stood where, ironically, the British Petroleum refinery is located today.

Because he was not officially a soldier in the American army, he did not qualify for a pension until a special act of Congress in 1864 granted him the amount of eight dollars a month for life. Peter Navarre died on March 20, 1874, in a hotel near the corner of Front and Main in East Toledo, and is buried at Mt. Carmel Cemetery in an unmarked grave. At the time of his death, he was president of the Maumee Valley Pioneer Association which later became the Maumee Valley Historical Society.

A monument in honor of Peter and his brother Robert was dedicated at Navarre Park on July 4, 1914. A cabin built late in the old scout's life by his sons was moved to Navarre Park on September 9th (Peter Navarre Day) in 1922. In 1957 it was taken to the Zoo, and then in the 1970s was moved to Toledo Botanical Gardens where it has been restored to look like an early pioneer homestead. A visit there today is a reminder of the earlier cabin Peter Navarre built nearly two hundred years ago when he came to the untouched forests of the East Side.

Navarre Cabin when at Navarre Park, 1945.

Portrait of Peter Nev...
The famous scout who
served in the ...
under Gen. ...

Chapter 2

TAMING THE WILDERNESS...

*

Early Pioneers

from

The Navarres

to

The Cholera Epidemic of 1854

*

WILD ANIMALS AND EAST SIDE PIONEERS

A hundred and fifty years ago, the land east of the Maumee River was largely covered by forest with only a few scattered settlements. Indians still lived out near the bay at Presque Isle, and many kinds of wild animals roamed through the dense woods that we now call East Toledo.

Stories told by the early pioneers mention an abundance of wild game. Robert Navarre said that his father had been known to kill twenty-one deer in a single week. Wolves wandering in packs of up to three hundred were also seen, as well as flocks of wild turkeys that covered an acre of ground.

It was Robert Navarre, later to become the range light keeper at Ironville, who also made the single greatest catch of fish recorded at that time. He told of bringing in 114 barrels of fish in just three hauls with a seine in 1858, with each barrel weighing 250 pounds. Even though fishermen were even then famous for exaggeration, Navarre's story was verified in Isaac Wright's well-known history of the East Side written in 1894.

Robert Gardner, who was elected Sheriff of Lucas County in 1916, grew up on the family farm on Pickle Road about a mile and a half past Willow Cemetery. He recalled the log house of his childhood that "usually had a deer or two hung up about the place, not to mention wild turkeys, partridge and all kinds of fish." He also told of the fish running so thick in the rapids of the Maumee that he would catch them merely by "putting a piece of red flannel on a hook and throwing the line into the river."

In 1838, Jacques Navarre killed a panther in the woods near his farm out on the Bay Shore. He had adopted an Indian boy who discovered its trail and traced the animal to a hollow log. After stopping up the log, the boy went home for help. Jacques and his brother Antoinne returned and chopped a hole in the log, and then shot the animal when the panther stuck its head out of the hole.

The last recorded instance of a deer being shot on the East Side was the one killed by Moses Dowell near Front and Oak Streets in 1873, two years after the first Franklin School was built. Also, Elijah Woodruff, another prominent early pioneer who settled in East Toledo in 1837, remembered a bear killing a calf at what is now the corner of Starr Avenue and Arden Place.

In addition to the threat of wild animals, those first pioneers also had to carve their homesteads out of the thick forests east of the river. Asa Maddocks, who came to Toledo in 1831, was typical of those hardy individuals. He not only worked for the old Toledo Gazette and started the Michigan Whig in Adrian, but he also joined the 49'ers in the famous gold rush to California. When he finally settled down for good, Mr. Maddocks started one of the first fruit tree nurseries in northwest Ohio. His orchards were in the area of Starr and Euclid, and extended all the way back to what is now Nevada Street.

Another pioneer was Elias Fassett, who built a homestead on Oak Street (near Fassett) where the East Side Hospital later stood. He recalled seeing the remnants of the pre-historic Indian fort on the bend of the river at Hathaway (originally called Fort) at Miami Street.

Some of the other hardy settlers east of the river were named Whitmore, Denman, Momany, Howland, Jennison, Prentice, Berry and Consaul. These rugged families, along with many others, coped with the wild animals, disease, and hard work necessary to lay the foundations for a community east of the Maumee that would boom only in the last years of the nineteenth century.

ELIZABETH NAVARRE: PIONEER WOMAN ON THE BAY SHORE

The stories Elizabeth Navarre told her grand-daughter, Helen Lang, have kept alive some memories from the early pioneer days on the East Side.

According to Elizabeth Navarre, when her family came to America from France in the 1700s, they settled in Canada because the allowed quota for French immigrants was already filled in the Colonies. Long before the taming of the Black Swamp, the Navarres came into a northern Ohio populated mostly by Indians with only a few trails winding through the vast uncharted forests. It was in this wilderness that the Navarres, especially Peter, proved so helpful to General William Henry Harrison and the American forces during the War of 1812.

For their services in the war, the Navarre family was given a large tract of land out along the Bay Shore. Elizabeth, the daughter of Peter's brother Alexis, grew up in a log cabin built about 1837 on a portion of the Navarre tract where Otter Creek Road joins Bay Shore Road, now occupied by the BP oil refinery.

Elizabeth, who was the youngest child in the family, remembered going with her older sister Sarah to milk the cows. Thick woods surrounded the farm, and the young girls expected to see an Indian hiding behind every cow they approached. The Indians, though, were usually friendly with the settlers. The family always kept the cabin unlocked, and on cold nights would often awake in the morning to find the living area crowded with Indian families sleeping on the floor by the fire.

Elizabeth recalled that when some of the Indians were sent off to Canada, the squaws asked the Navarre girls to look after the graves of their loved ones who were buried in the woods along the bay. Some of the gifts, like beaded sewing-needle cases, that the Indians gave to the Navarre children have been passed down through the years in the family.

One time the two girls found a baby deer in the woods. They were not allowed to keep it as a pet because it belonged in the wild, but when the deer was full-grown it would often visit the house.

It would come right up to the door and lick the frame, looking to find salt.

Elizabeth Navarre married Cad Williams, who also owned land along Bay Shore Road. While still a young bride, she was left alone when her husband went off to fight in the Civil War. He was captured by the Confederates and sent to the notorious Andersonville Prison in Georgia. Elizabeth recalled his daring escape.

The prisoners were served their food in tin cans, and her husband was able to use those cans to dig a crude tunnel out of his cell and make his escape. Alone deep in Confederate territory, his only chance was to hide away on a train heading north. He had prepared himself by lying awake listening to train whistles until he could tell which trains would take him in the right direction.

After successfully hopping a north-bound train, he spent several days on a flat-bed car exposed to the elements. By the time he finally reached Ohio he was severely burned by the sun. It was a tattered, bearded, sun-bleached man who knocked at the door of the house on Bay Shore Road. When Elizabeth opened the door, she shouted, "Go away, Tramp!" She did not even recognize her own husband.

Elizabeth and Cad lived the rest of their lives out on the Bay Shore. Their youngest child, Thad, born in 1878, married Lena Mominee and also settled on Bay Shore Road. Elizabeth survived well into the 20th century, and she lived with Thad's family in her old age. Helen Lang was Thad and Lena's daughter. Her memories of her grandmother, Elizabeth Navarre, bring back the way life was for those early pioneer families who settled in the area that became the East Side.

CENTENNIAL DINNER HONORS EAST SIDE PIONEERS

On Toledo's 100th birthday in 1937, a dinner reunion was held to honor East Siders who had lived east of the river for fifty years or more. It was probably the largest single gathering of those who contributed most to the growth and development of East Toledo.

The event was sponsored by the East Toledo Club and held at the club meeting rooms at 307 Main Street. The dinner was at noon, followed by an "old-timers' meeting" from 2:00 to 5:00. It was reported that many who attended were "choked with emotion" and some wept to be with friends again that they had not seen for so many years.

Paul Coney, a past president of the East Toledo Club, was general chairman of the event, and the Club's first president, Nolan Boggs, served as toastmaster. Dr. A. J. Townsend, history professor at the University of Toledo, was the guest speaker. The Bay Shore Pioneer Club, led by Thad Williams, and the Oregon Township Club also sent representatives. Various prizes and honors were given.

The oldest person attending the dinner was Celeste Gladieux, who celebrated his 90th birthday only the day before. He was given an electric lamp. Mrs. Nellie Rogers was the oldest person at the reunion, topping everyone at a still active age of 93. She was the widow of Captain Romeyn Rogers, the first person from the East Side to enlist in response to President Lincoln's call for troops at the beginning of the Civil War.

For entertainment, Henry Ehrle, a native East Sider, sang to the accompaniment of William Clifton. Fred Murphy, an "old time fiddler," was said to have "enlivened the pioneers." As part of the program, several prominent businessmen were introduced, including Henry Thibodeau, L. E. Flory, George Parks, D. Harry Harpster, and E. J. Smith. Alex and William Navarre were honored as descendants of the War of 1812 scouts Peter and Robert Navarre.

Several of the pioneers recalled the early days on the East Side. James Dupont remembered talking with Peter Navarre. He said that Mr. Navarre was never too busy to spend time with the children who lived near his home on the Bay Shore. Mrs. Gottlieb Yenzer also recalled those early days when Indians still roamed the woods of East Toledo.

D. M. O'Sullivan, retired police captain, was unable to attend because of health problems, but sent a letter which told of his coming to the East Side as a boy. He recalled at that time East Toledo was nearly all forest, with only a few houses along the River Road (Miami Street) and on First Street.

William Berry told the assembly that his mother, Mrs. Mary Berry, was the first teacher on the East Side. The small schoolhouse stood on the river-bank where Consaul Street now joins Front, long before Tony Packo's occupied the site. Her school opened in 1837, and Mrs. Berry boarded with the families of her students and received a weekly salary of $1.50.

The list of those who attended the centennial reads like a roll call of memorable East Side families: Consaul, Lamb, Messer, Navarre, Gladieux, Flory Eggleston, Tracy, Gradel, Redd, Reddish, Ordway, Rogers, Drouillard, Berry, and many more. It is unfortunate that camcorders were not around to preserve all the memories of those gathered pioneers. But for one day, on Toledo's 100th anniversary, time was set aside to remember the early days and to honor those who had contributed so much to the development and growth of the East Side.

PIONEERS OF OREGON TOWNSHIP

Early records from the 1880s found in the archives of the Oregon-Jerusalem Historical Society list many of the pioneers who first settled Oregon Township. Some of the more familiar names are described below.

Isaac Clay was born in Center County, Pennsylvania, on February 9, 1813, and came to Ohio at the age of four. In 1830 he moved to Wood County and married Jane Ann Tompkins six years later. She had five children before her early death, and Mr. Clay's second wife, Lucinda Myers, had six children.

One of the first to arrive in Oregon Township was Nathan Gardner, who came into the area in 1831 from New York. He had eight sons and two daughters. During the Civil War he enlisted with the 130th Ohio Regiment. Like most of the pioneers, he spent his life farming. Morrison Drive used to be called Gardner Street after this family.

Another very early arrival was Peter Momany, who came to Oregon Township in 1836 at the age of nine with his parents Anthony and Angeline Momany. He served in the 130th Ohio Infantry during the Civil War. One year later, in 1837, Wesley Hicks came to the Township with his parents Lawson and Eleanor (Merritt) Hicks. He had three sons, and held many Township offices including Justice of the Peace for several years.

Henry Cook, born in Jackson, Michigan in 1841, arrived in Oregon Township in 1854. He enlisted in the 14th Ohio Infantry at the age of 20, and later served in the 30th Ohio Cavalry. After the war he married Elizabeth McCullough and had seven children.

Another early settler, in 1847, was George Bury. He was born in Germany on April 4, 1813. He married Ann Catherine Johlin in 1850, and the couple also had seven children.

Stephen Rideout (born 1806) and Thomas Rideout (born 1824) both arrived from England in 1844. Stephen married Maria Stainer and had one child; Thomas had six children.

Two of the first children born in Oregon Township were Perry Coy (March 31, 1850) and Horace Coy (November 21, 1852). Their father died in the cholera epidemic of 1854. Both later farmed along the road named for the Coy family. Horace was a Township Trustee and School Director.

Two brothers born in the Township even earlier were George Smithlin (April 23, 1847) and Mathew Smithlin (February 4, 1849). Both had four children and farmed between Navarre Avenue and Pickle Road out past the Coy farms. The Mathew Smithlin house (c. 1870) still stands on Coy Road.

Joseph Gladieux was born in France on September 2, 1818, and came to America when he was fifteen. He came to Oregon Township in 1849 and had eleven children. His home still stands at the northeast corner of Wheeling and Pickle Road.

Peter Heider, born in Germany in 1819, came to the Township in 1851. He also was a farmer and had eleven children by two wives. Another German farmer, John Klotz, arrived the following year and had six children by his wife Lena Elk.

Others who settled in Oregon Township during the 1850s were Jacob Muller, B. Miller, Joseph Phillips, Trayton Moon, C. Steiger, Henry Wilhelm, Julian Dubois, James Crofts, and Fred Joehlin (at the age of 3). The Johlin Winery on Corduroy Road has been in business for over 100 years and the family home dates to 1870.

In 1861, John Klag (born in 1824 in Bavaria) moved to Toledo from Perrysburg. The next year he became pastor of St. Marcus German Lutheran Church on Grasser Street. The old part of the church, now called First St. Mark's, was built in 1863. Rev. Klag had nine children by two wives.

Christian Schneider, a gardener, was born in Germany on December 10, 1832, and settled in Oregon Township in 1868. That year he married Anna Mister, and they had six children. The Schneider house still stands at the northwest corner of Pickle Road and Grasser Street near Brandville School.

These and many other pioneer families, such as the Moshers, Messers, Fassetts, and of course the Navarres, each played an important role in taming the swamp and settling the land east of the river that is now the municipality of Oregon.

PIONEER FAMILIES OF ROSSFORD

Rossford got its name from glass-maker Edward Ford and his wife Caroline Ross. When Mr. Ford came to the east shore of the Maumee in 1898, "Golden Rule" Jones was Mayor of Toledo, a large house could be built for $750, and a beef dinner cost a dime. However, this was relatively late in the history of the area that became known as Rossford.

Long before Mr. Ford produced his first plate-glass there on October 28, 1899, the area was the home of early settlers who could remember when wolves and Indians roamed the forests along the river. In his book The Roots Grow Deep, William Earl Aiken traces the history of some of those pioneer families.

Gabriel Crane, born in the year 1800, heard tales as a boy about a land of rich soil along "a river they call the Maumee." At the age of twenty, Crane walked all the way to Perrysburg from New York state, crossing the Black Swamp where Route 20 is today. He sampled the soil as far as Maumee Bay, and following the old custom of his father, even tasted the good rich dirt.

The taste must have been satisfactory, because Crane soon began buying land from the government, until he owned hundreds of acres along the river from Oregon Road to where the LOF plant now stands. He was a friend of Peter Navarre, and he built the first frame house in the area on the later site of the Thermopane plant. In his fifties, he helped lay brick during the building of the Oliver House, which still stands on the Middlegrounds. Gabriel Crane lived to the age of 82, and is buried in Willow Cemetery.

Crane's daughter, Clara, who was born in 1841, lived long enough to sell some land to Edward Ford. One evening when she was a new bride sewing by the fire, she looked up and saw an Indian staring at her through the window. She also remembered that her father hunted wolves, gladly risking his life for the pelts because they sold at the high price of $1.25. One of Crane's sons, James, built the large brick house on Miami Street where the LOF Oldtimers held their annual picnic for many years.

A grandson, Carl Crane, remembered the coming of the Ford Glass Works. He also happened to be close by one day when a tire blew out on Mr. Ford's chocolate brown Peerless. At a signal from the chauffeur, young Crane was eager to help change the tire. Dusty all over from wrestling with the old clincher rim, he heard a deep voice say, "Son, come here and hold out your hand." He was astounded at the coins poured into his hand, more money than the boy had ever seen. Edward Ford had given him 75 cents!

Another early pioneer was Doria Tracy (1808-1894), who came to the area in 1867 and settled along Grassy Creek where Eagle Point Road now turns toward the river. He ran a prosperous lumber business. His son William built a large home where the Catholic Church now stands in Rossford, and he became widely known for his orchards.

Doria Tracy's daughter Katharine married Julius Lamson, a co-founder of the Lamson Brothers Company. When he was a young clerk boarding on Summit Street, Julius used to row across the river to court his future bride. After their wedding in 1878, they lived on Miami Street just north of Oakdale (then called Brown Road).

Elliott Warner (1844-1930), another pioneer, arrived in 1875 and bought land now occupied by Rossford High School. Warner, also a successful fruit grower, taught Sunday School in the red schoolhouse that stood at the corner of Eagle Point and the River Road. A Civil War veteran and graduate of Oberlin College, Mr. Warner served several terms as a Ross Township trustee.

Another early settler was George Davis. In 1856 he built a house on open farm land. Over forty

William Tracy Homestead, Now Site of Catholic Church.

years later, when the streets of Rossford were platted, his house became 156 Bacon Street.

Rossford of course has long been known for its important role as a producer of plate-glass. Not many people, however, remember those first pioneer families who settled the land and cleared the forests in the days before the coming of Caroline Ross and Edward Ford.

ELIJAH WOODRUFF: EAST SIDE PATRIARCH

Many people remember the names of prominent early Toledoans such as Peter Navarre, Jessup Scott, Benjamin Stickney, and David Ross Locke. However, one important pioneer, whose life spanned the entire 19th century, is often overlooked. Elijah Woodruff was truly a patriarchal figure, and it was common practice for East Siders to measure the history of their area in terms of his lifetime.

Mr. Woodruff was born early in Thomas Jefferson's presidency, was a teenager when Napoleon met his Waterloo, was nearly sixty when the Civil War began, and yet he was still alive to witness the assassination of William McKinley and to welcome the arrival of the 20th century. All told, his life spanned the terms of twenty-four presidents.

Elijah J. Woodruff was born in Watertown, Connecticut, in 1802. He first came to Toledo in 1833, and settled on the East Side in 1837. As a young man he worked as a timber contractor and farmed on the Bissell land. He prospered and was appointed the first Postmaster of Utah, as East Toledo was then called.

Being Postmaster was not an easy job in those early days, and Mr. Woodruff himself often had to bring the mail across the river in a row boat. It is no wonder he was a leader in establishing a regular ferry system on the Maumee during the 1850s.

In 1852 Mr. Woodruff built a fine home noted for its walnut timbers and perpendicular weatherboarding near the present corner of Euclid and Starr Avenue. It was moved to 12 Garfield Place about the turn of the century. As the finest house of its time in East Toledo, it played a role in the cholera epidemic of 1854. Mr. Woodruff survived that severe epidemic and went on to hold many public offices in East Toledo and Oregon Township.

On many occasions, Indians visited Mr. Woodruff's home. He once said, "I always found the Indians very honest in their dealings. The squaws were a nuisance by their begging, but they never stole anything." He recalled cold winter nights in his old log house when the floor was "so covered with Indians that some of them were sleeping under my bed, and the next day the house would need a good fumigation." He also made them leave their ponies outside.

One cold night an Indian family stopped at his door with six-month-old twins. The babies were so cold that the mother covered them with ashes from the fireplace so they could get to sleep.

Mr. Woodruff was also active in the branch of the underground railroad that went through Toledo. Along with Ezra Howland and Oliver Brown, he would feed runaway slaves and ferry them across the river to Stickney's Point, near Brush Street, on their way to safety in Canada.

The danger involved for those on the underground railroad increased when the Fugitive Slave Bill was passed. It imposed a fine of $3,000 and two years penal servitude on anyone caught harboring or aiding a slave. Yet Mr. Woodruff continued to help the slaves escape, often hiding them in the heavy thickets along the river near where the Edison Acme plant is today.

In the early days, wild animals and many deer roamed the East Side of the river, a welcome source of food for the pioneer families. By all accounts, Mr. Woodruff was not much of a hunter, but he liked to tell of getting one deer—by drowning it in the river. He recalled, "I had heard the Indians and French hunters often tell how to catch a deer in the water. They catch them by the tail and just raise them up enough so that the head will go under water. If you raise the hind part any higher the deer would be liable to kick the boat to pieces."

A big celebration was held in honor of Mr. Woodruff's 100th birthday on September 18, 1902. The event, which took place at Navarre Park, was organized by Postmaster William H. Tucker, Father

Patrick O'Brien of Good Shepherd, and printer Isaac
Wright. Among the pioneers who came to honor Mr.
Woodruff were Louis Metzger, Elias Fassett, Robert
Navarre, John Thorp, Captain Romeyn Rogers, George
Scheets, and J. C. Messer.

　　　Elijah Woodruff died peacefully in his sleep on
January 7, 1904. But he still has an important
connection to the East Side. In an interesting twist
of history, Jeff Eversman, who was the organizer of
the East Toledo Historical Society and who
discovered many of these facts about Mr. Woodruff's
life, has learned that through a common ancestor in
Connecticut Jeff and Mr. Woodruff are fifth cousins
five times removed.

Elijah Woodruff.

Perhaps no other single life has typified all the changes that took place on the East Side and what life was like for pioneers such as Elijah Woodruff who settled there during the 19th century.

THE CHOLERA EPIDEMIC OF 1854

Today when Fourth of July celebrations are planned, rain is the biggest threat to ruin the occasion. In 1854, an elaborate picnic prepared for the Fourth was ruined by a much more serious enemy--an outbreak of the cholera.

Cholera, a highly contagious bacterial disease that attacks the digestive system, has been tamed by modern medicine. In the 19th century, however, it was often fatal, claiming the lives of thousands of people, including the poet Gerard Manley Hopkins and the 12th President of the United States, Zachary Taylor. Cholera cemeteries once dotted the countryside, because victims were often buried together in isolated areas to avoid contamination.

According to Isaac Wright's book, The East Side, there were outbreaks of cholera in the Maumee Valley as early as 1830. One death was officially recorded in 1849, and in 1852 Michael Horton died of the disease on the Charles Coy farm.

But in late June 1854, a passenger steamer from Buffalo landed at the Peckham & Berdan warehouse at the foot of Lagrange Street. That night, as people from the boat camped around bonfires on shore, one of them suddenly took sick and died. The disease quickly spread and soon reached epidemic proportions.

On Saturday, July 1st, preparations were

being made to celebrate the coming holiday in grand
style. East Siders planned to have a large picnic in
a grove on the property of Elijah Woodruff near
what is now Euclid and Starr Avenue. Pies, cakes,
boiled hams, and all the "fixins" were stored in Mr.
Woodruff's two-year-old house, probably the largest
home on the East Side at the time. Long tables were
built under the oaks, and swings were hung for the
children. Everything was ready, Wright tells us, for
"a grand jollification."

Elijah Woodruff House, built 1852.

The Fourth of July dawned bright and clear,
but there was no celebration. The grove remained
empty and the food spoiled in Elijah Woodruff's
deserted house. On July 2nd and 3rd the cholera
had spread to the East Side, and twenty-seven
people had already died in that part of Oregon
Township known as Utah.

Victor Plumey died on Sunday morning. Riding to the cemetery, Nelson Smith remarked, "Poor Vic is gone; I wonder which of us will go next?" At 8:00 on Monday morning, Louis Metzger, Smith's traveling companion the previous day, buried Smith under an apple tree near the corner of Oak Street and Starr Avenue. Mr. Metzger left town that same day.

Many were able to escape to the countryside, as in the great plague of London in 1665, but others were not so fortunate. The death toll mounted in East Toledo: a cobbler who had a little shop on Oak Street, two unknown immigrants laid side by side in unmarked graves. As many as thirty people were buried in that makeshift cemetery under the apple tree, where Franklin School playground now stands, even at that time a favorite play area for children.

As the number of deaths continued to grow, one life was unexpectedly spared. According to Isaac Wright's account, a greedy undertaker, who was paid by the city for the number of burials he made, often would deposit the body into the ground without the coffin, which could then be used again. Returning one time to the cemetery, the undertaker saw his previous cholera burial sitting on the fence. The "victim" had only been drunk. Not being buried in a coffin had saved the man's life.

With the spread of the disease, deaths were being recorded in all areas of the East Side from the Bay Shore to Perrysburg. In The Perrysburg Story, Ardath Danford tells of the suffering inflicted on that community from which the cholera had claimed as many as 120 people by mid-August. Seth Bruce made coffins in a hallway of the Court House. And a guard was posted on the bridge to Maumee to prevent anyone from coming or going between the two towns.

Dr. Erasmus Peck has been called the hero of

the epidemic in Perrysburg. He left the doors of his drug store open day and night so that people could get the medicine they needed. He also continued to unselfishly care for the sick, even after his partner, Dr. James Robertson, contracted the disease and died. In addition to Dr. Robertson, who left a wife and two small children, many other leading citizens were lost, including Exchange Hotel owner Jarvis Spafford, Elijah Huntington, Mrs. Asher Cook, Rebecca Webb McKnight, and Dr. Peck's mother.

Proportionally, the East Side was devastated even more than Perrysburg. Of the 175 residents living in what became the 6th Ward of Toledo, over one-third of them perished in the epidemic of 1854. Included among the names of the dead were members of the most prominent families: Prentice, Plumey, Coy, Rogers, Brown, Messer, and many more.

One interesting result of the epidemic was an attempt to change the name of the river. Some people thought the name Maumee was so much associated with disease that settlers would not come to the area. The name "Grand Rapids River" was proposed. In addition, for a short time, the city of Maumee was called "South Toledo." But the only change that lasted was the little town of Gilead took on the proposed name for the river and became known as Grand Rapids.

In the long run, the most beneficial result of the epidemic was the increased demand to drain the Black Swamp, even though the swamp was innocent of the cholera. Twenty years later, major drainage programs began and the swamp was transformed into the area's most fertile farmland.

Chapter 3

*

The East Side

during

The Civil War

from

1861-1865

*

A CIVIL WAR RAIDER FROM THE EAST SIDE

At 6:15 on the day after Christmas in 1916, Wilson W. Brown, one of the last surviving members of the famous Andrews Raiders, died quietly in his home at 874 Forsythe Street in East Toledo. Brown had played an important part in perhaps the most celebrated Union raid behind the Confederate lines during the whole Civil War.

Because of the great danger, only volunteers were asked to make the raid deep into Confederate territory. Those twenty-two volunteers from three

Ohio regiments were placed under the command of James A. Andrews.

Wilson Brown's Home, 874 Forsythe St.

The plan involved stealing a train to ride north tearing up tracks, telegraph lines, and bridges between Atlanta and Chattanooga, thus severing a vital Confederate line of communications.

Disguised as civilians, Andrews and his men infiltrated Confederate lines as far south as Marietta, Georgia, near Atlanta. There, on Saturday, April 12, 1862, the raiders stole a Rebel train called the "General" while its crew was nearby eating breakfast. Some sources claim Mr. Brown had the distinction of being the engineer of the train as it raced north toward Chattanooga.

The men calmly stopped only a mile up the

track to destroy telegraph lines, tear up some rails, and refuel. Unknown to the raiders, however, the Confederates had already discovered the train was missing and were pursuing frantically on foot. Led by conductor William Fuller, they found a handcar, which they used until they came to the torn up track. They continued on foot until they located another train, the "Texas," and then the chase began in earnest.

Meanwhile, the raiders had been stopping several times to cut telegraph wires, and were not aware of their pursuers until they heard the whistle of the "Texas" coming up behind them. The chase now grew so hot that the raiders had no time to destroy the vital Confederate bridges. They were too busy trying to slow down their enemies.

They tried piling ties across the tracks, but the "Texas" merely brushed them aside. They attempted to set a boxcar on fire with shavings and send it back down on their pursuers. But it had begun to rain and the car would not ignite. Finally, about ninety miles north of Atlanta, the "General" ran out of fuel and the raiders fled on foot into the woods.

After a week-long manhunt using tracking-dogs, all the raiders were captured. Andrews and seven other raiders were hanged on June 2, 1862. The rest were imprisoned in Atlanta. Fourteen prisoners, including Wilson Brown, managed to break jail by overpowering the guards. Six of them were recaptured and exchanged for Confederate prisoners nearly a year later. Mr. Brown and seven others were able to escape and eventually make it to the Union lines.

All in all, the raiders had done little damage that was not easily repaired. But the gallantry of the raid fired patriotism in the North during those darkest days of the Civil War, and Andrews' Raid

became a symbol of Union daring against overwhelming odds. For their bravery, the raiders were
personally awarded by President Lincoln the first
Congressional Medals of Honor ever issued by the
United States of America.

In a small churchyard southeast of Toledo
near Luckey, Ohio, Wilson Brown is buried. His
house on Forsythe Street in East Toledo is still
standing, but gives no hint of its former occupant's
dramatic involvement in our nation's history.

REMEMBERING THE FORD POST, G.A.R.

The Ford Post, G.A.R. (Grand Army of the
Republic), was the veterans' organization of East
Siders who fought in the Civil War. The Ford Post
monument, dedicated in 1882, still stands in Willow
Cemetery, commemorating a proud organization which
was responsible for many community improvements
east of the river.

The Post was named in honor of Captain Hyatt
Ford, an East Side man who had organized Co. B,
67th Regiment, Ohio Volunteer Infantry. Captain
Ford was killed in action at the battle of Winchester
on March 23, 1862, during Stonewall Jackson's
campaign in the Shenandoah Valley.

The official organization of the Ford Post took
place on January 21st, 1867, in the meeting rooms of
old Bronson's Hall at Front and Oak Streets. General
John H. Kountz, General J. Kent Hamilton, and Capt.
Hall were the chief organizers. Politics crept in,
however, and the Post was disbanded for a time.

In 1878 it was re-organized with more broad-
minded goals, and thus would continue to serve East

Siders as an active force in the community until the 1920s. The Ford Post had 165 members in 1894 and 144 members in 1908, which was the time of the National G.A.R. Encampment held in Toledo. By 1929, there were still thirteen surviving members living on the East Side.

That year, on June 7th, the East Toledo Club gave a luncheon in honor of those Civil War soldiers who had gone off to fight 67 years before. The seven surviving veterans who were able to attend the luncheon were: J. L. Barrett, Jacob Confer, John Washington, W. B. Moorhead, John Cupp, A. J. Young, and A. R. Fassett.

At the celebration, Superintendent of Schools Charles Meek gave a speech about Abraham Lincoln and the Civil War. He told of Lincoln's quarrels with the reluctant Commander of the Union Army, George B. McClellan. General McClellan would not engage Lee's army, but instead pestered the President even about the "disposition" of some dairy cows he had captured. Lincoln penned the famous reply: "George, milk them." Meek also quoted from Lincoln's sympathetic letter to a mother who had lost five sons in the war.

The Ford Post also had a ladies auxiliary, the Ford Circle, which was organized in 1880, and for over fifty years participated in the annual Memorial Day services. Another patriotic service organization grew from the Ford Post, G.A.R.: the Ford Post Cadets. Later, at the time of the Spanish-American War, the Cadets became part of the National Guard.

As a civic organization, the Ford Post was helpful in bringing many improvements to the East Side. New sewers and streets, the expansion of streetcar lines, and the opening of new housing additions were only some of the developments promoted by those influential veterans.

Although the last East Side veteran who actually fought in the Civil War has been dead for over fifty years now, the work of the Ford Post should not be forgotten. The monument in Willow Cemetery is more than a war memorial. It also commemorates those who helped the East Side grow long after the armies laid down their arms at Appomattox.

THE FORD POST HISTORY OF THE CIVIL WAR

Toledoans interested in the Civil War can find a special treasure in the local history room of the downtown Toledo Public Library. It is the large, handwritten volume of "Personal War Sketches" of the Ford Post, G.A.R. This huge book comes in its own "suitcase" and contains the memories of all the East Side veterans who fought in the Civil War.

This valuable book was originally presented to the Ford Post in 1892 by veterans George Scheets, Frank Wilson, Sylvester Brown, William Finlay, and Joseph Ford. The entire collection of individual reminiscences was transcribed by Captain Scheets, who served a brief term as Mayor of Toledo in 1884 and who lived in a house still standing at the corner of Euclid and Starr Avenue.

In addition to being Mayor, he also worked for many years in the Lucas County Treasurer's office. He lived to be 86 years old, dying quietly in his home on February 9th, 1929. The remarkable book that he penned preserves the thrilling stories told by those who actually took part in the largest battles ever fought on this continent.

Captain Scheets himself fought throughout the Civil War, entering the Union Army as a private and retiring as a Captain. He participated in the battles of Stones River, Chickamauga (where Toledoan Gen. Steedman won fame), Atlanta, and went with Sherman on his famous march to the sea. He listed General Sherman and General George Thomas as the greatest leaders he served under.

The Ford Post history records the death of Hyatt Ford and the memories of those who knew him. It also gives Wilson Brown's account of his participation in Andrews' "ill-fated" Raid. He tells of his escape from prison and the suffering of "much privation" to reach the safety of the Union lines.

Among other adventures of East Side veterans recorded in the Ford Post volume are those recalled by Henry Crane. Captain Crane was one of Hyatt Ford's closest friends who later became Commander of the Ford Post. After the war he operated a large greenhouse near Miami Street and Oregon Road, and also served on the Board of Education.

Captain Crane recalled being wounded at the battle of Fort Wagner, South Carolina. On July 18, 1863, he took a "musketball in the thigh." He recovered, however, to see further action, and was present during the final battles around Petersburg and Richmond.

Michael Burgermeister was with the 68th Regiment, Ohio Infantry Volunteers, and fought in many of the bloodiest engagements of the war. At Shiloh he served under Lew Wallace, the General who came to Grant's rescue and who later wrote the famous novel Ben-Hur. Burgermeister was disabled in 1862, but re-enlisted in 1864 and was present during the Grand Review of the Army in Washington when the war ended.

Another Ford Post member, Richard Lang, described in the book the deadly fighting in the Wilderness, or the "half acre of death," during

Grant's "on to Richmond" campaign on 1864. Lang was also at the ensuing battle of Spotsylvania Court House where some of the fiercest fighting of the war took place at the "angle of the devil," later called Bloody Angle.

Lang told how he was at "the stand in the breastworks on the Weldon Road where the whole of our Division fell back when the rebels charged." Only the Companies of his Regiment "held the works until the enemy was repulsed." At the Smithsonian in Washington is the stump of a tree chopped down solely by the massed hail of bullets concentrated on Lang's position at this "angle of the devil."

In all, there were 116 eye-witness accounts of the war recorded by Captain Scheets in this history given to the Ford Post. All the major battles are mentioned, and many of the soldiers recalled being wounded or taken prisoner. These Civil War stories of bravery and sacrifice show that East Siders participated fully in the fiercest conflict ever fought on American soil.

When the tired soldiers of both armies returned home, the country was ready to rebuild. The year the war ended, the first bridge was built across the Maumee River and a decade later began the boom years on the East Side that would last until well into the 20th century.

THE LAST CIVIL WAR VETERAN FROM THE EAST SIDE

When Dr. Albert J. Marks died at the old East Side Hospital in 1942, he was the last surviving member of the Ford Post, G.A.R., the last East Side veteran who had fought in the Civil War. He was 100 years old at the time of his death.

Dr. Marks was the youngest of eight children and was born in New York City where his parents had settled after arriving from England. The family moved to Ohio when he was still very young. One of his earliest Ohio memories was his mother making him wear an apron to school. When the other children made fun of him, he left the apron on a gatepost, preferring punishment to ridicule.

His long life goes back to the canal era in the early history of the Maumee Valley. As a young man, Dr. Marks was assistant collector for the Miami & Erie Canal at Maumee under L. T. Clark, and later under Samuel Galloway in Toledo. He also served as collector for the middle district of the Ohio Canal between Columbus and Coshocton.

Soon after the Civil War broke out, Dr. Marks enlisted in the 128th Regiment, Ohio Volunteer Infantry. For a while he was assigned to guard the Confederate prisoners kept at Johnson's Island. His favorite memory of the Civil War was that in the important presidential election of 1864, he was old enough to cast his vote for Abraham Lincoln.

When the war was over, Dr. Marks found medicine an irresistible calling. After serving a required two-year apprenticeship, he attended a medical college in Cincinnati, graduating in 1880. He first practiced medicine in Wood County and then in Millbury before moving to Toledo in 1889. His wife, Mary Ann, also studied medicine, and when Dr. Marks was a professor at the Physio-Medica College of Chicago, his signature appeared on his wife's 1888 diploma.

Not only the husband and wife, but a son, Arthur, and daughter, Maud, also followed the medical profession. The family experienced tragedy, however, when Mary Ann died in 1900 and Arthur followed in 1913. Dr. Maud Marks, though, continued her practice for many years at 1130 Starr Avenue in the same office as her father, who was still going strong at the age of 92, when failing eyesight finally forced him to retire.

Dr. Marks not only practiced medicine past his 90th birthday, but also continued to operate his car. Even after retirement, he remained active in the Ford Post, and was one of the oldest Masons in the country.

When he was 99 years old, Dr. Marks fell and fractured a hip. But he was still strong enough to celebrate his 100th birthday with a large party held at the home of his nurse, Mrs. Dora Larmie, at 1018 Forsythe Street. Dr. Marks died soon afterward, taking with him the memories of the last East Sider to have personally fought in the Civil War.

Ford Post Monument, Willow Cemetery.

Chapter 4

ON THE STREET WHERE YOU LIVE...

*

East Side Growth and Development

from

The First Bridge

to

The Turn of the Century

*

THE HISTORY OF TOLEDO'S FIRST BRIDGE

The Cherry Street Bridge, recently renamed the Martin Luther King Jr. Bridge, has had a long and interesting history. Although it has experienced several transformations, the bridge between Cherry Street and what is now Main Street on the East Side has served Toledoans well for over 125 years, ever since the first Cherry Street Bridge was built at the end of the Civil War.

Until August 1865, the only way to cross the Maumee River was by boat. Several ferry operators, such as Elijah Woodruff and Captain M. T. Huntley, prospered during the 1840s and 50s. In fact, there was some reluctance to build a bridge at all. The City Council passed a resolution stating that a bridge to the East Side would be "unwise and inexpedient and likely to produce a paramount injury to the commercial advantages of the City."

Even after it was built, the first Cherry Street Bridge was unpopular because of the high tolls: two cents per person, a half-cent for pigs and goats, and as much as 25 cents for a carriage and two horses. The first wooden structure, built close to the water, needed frequent repairs, and horses that passed over it at more than a walk would tear up the unstable planking.

Unlike the current Ohio Turnpike, however, the tolls lasted for less than ten years, when public outcry convinced the city to purchase the 2,200 foot span from the Toledo Bridge Company and to make extensive repairs during the 1870s. Then in February 1883, ice floes carried away large sections of the bridge. Several East Side congregations, such as Sacred Heart and St. Mark's, were formed at this time, because people could not cross the river to attend church.

In 1884 the bridge was almost completely rebuilt with steel at a higher level above the water. This second Cherry Street Bridge was capable of supporting heavier traffic, including the streetcars that connected with the four East Toledo lines.

But tragedy struck again in 1908 when ice tore the steamer Yuma, loaded with flax seed, from its moorings and sent it crashing into the bridge. The large section on the west side of the river destroyed by the steamer was replaced with a temporary wooden span, while talk of building a sturdier modern bridge increased.

Second Cherry Street Bridge.

Two years earlier, in 1906, City Council had authorized a $525,000 bond issue for a new bridge, but the matter became tied up in the courts for several years. Finally, in 1913 the stone piers of steel-reinforced concrete were laid and the third Cherry Street Bridge was completed the following year.

Work on the new bridge was supervised by Ralph Modjeski, who was considered to be one of the finest structural engineers in the country. At the same time, the undamaged parts of the old bridge were floated down the river to become the Ash-Consaul Bridge, which survived until 1957.

Originally, four large towers were planned to contain the machinery, but the cost of the bridge had already reached $1,265,000 and funds had run out. As a result, for the next 25 years the lift mechanism was housed in small wooden shacks that

Mayor Brand Whitlock referred to as "those dog huts."

The bridge, however, was well received by the public. Harper's Magazine in 1914 printed a picture and called it "an instance of some of the wonderful things the cities are doing in these days, one of the great architectural achievements of the present time."

At first, the lift spans were operated by steam engines whose boilers had to be kept going 24 hours a day. It took four workers to operate the two lift controls, the boilers, the lanterns, and the manual traffic crossing gates. In the early days special care had to be used in halting horses, who on occasion, frightened by the noise of the machinery, would bolt forward and plunge through the widening gap to their deaths in the river below.

In time, the steam boilers were replaced by electricity, and today the 150-ton lift spans have computerized controls. This third Cherry Street Bridge has continued to be upgraded during its 75-year history, and a few years ago its name was changed to honor civil rights leader Martin Luther King, Jr.

Several other bridges now span the river: the Anthony Wayne or "Hi-Level" arches impressively 106 feet above the water, and the often-repaired Craig Bridge (I-280) and the DiSalle Bridge (I-75) have replaced the earlier Ash-Consaul and Fassett Street (1895-1957) bridges.

But even after 127 years, Toledo's first bridge continues to serve its citizens well, and when it was built it signaled the beginning of a period of rapid growth during the boom years of the East Side.

TOLEDOAN ADVANCED Y-BRIDGE ACROSS THE MAUMEE

Harvey Platt, pioneer Toledo lawyer and real estate dealer, went to his grave trying to convince city officials to build a Y-Bridge across the Maumee River. He envisioned a bridge anchored at Main Street in East Toledo that split in the middle of the river to join the west bank at both Cherry and Jackson streets. As was often the case, however, no one would listen to Mr. Platt's ideas.

Born in Essex County, New York, in 1827, Harvey Platt studied law and was admitted to the bar after moving to Cleveland in 1851 where he became clerk of the first probate court of Cuyahoga County. In 1855 he went to South America and two years later to Panama where he promoted artificial gas companies. He arrived here in 1859 and immediately became "a prominent figure in the development of Toledo."

Mr. Platt was influential in persuading the City Council to finance the first Cherry Street Bridge. He also saw the need for better marine development, and in 1869 secured the establishment of the present harbor lines on the south side of the river. In 1893, he was one of the national commissioners from Ohio to the World's Columbian Exposition in Chicago where he could publicize and promote this growing city on the Maumee River.

Even though Mr. Platt continued to live on his original homestead at 318 Chestnut Street, he always remained interested in the welfare of the East Side.

By 1900, no one owned more land in East Toledo than Mr. Platt. He built the Platt Building, later Caldwell Rambler, on land he owned at Front and Main where a McDonald's now stands. Also, it was Mr. Platt who sold to the city at a greatly reduced price all the land for Waite High School and Ravine Park.

Platt Street was of course "platted" on his land holdings, as was the street named after his wife, Mary Oswald, whom he married the year he arrived in Toledo. It is appropriate that their marriage of 47 years is reflected in the two streets that still run parallel their entire length.

Mr. Platt began his fight for a Y-Bridge in 1906 when he was nearly 80 years old. During his legal career he had already gained a rather contentious reputation. In fact, his friend L. E. Flory recalled that Mr. Platt would sometimes pretend to argue against whatever position he really favored, because city officials often voted against anything he proposed just to spite him.

He was asked why at his age he was still fighting so hard for issues such as the new bridge he envisioned. Mr. Platt replied, "Young man, I get my pleasure and my recreation out of fighting. I could not sit down, and remain quiet and idle. This bridge battle gives me the keenest satisfaction. I enjoy every move that is made. It's chess to me. It is my work, and I get my greatest pleasure out of my work."

But in spite of Mr. Platt's repeated legal efforts, the new Cherry Street Bridge was of conventional design rather than his proposed "Y" structure. He did not live to see it completed in 1914. He died at the age of 83 in 1910, and his funeral eulogy was given by Mayor Brand Whitlock. Harvey Platt did not get the bridge he wanted, but he certainly left his mark on the future development of the East Side.

EAST TOLEDO'S MAIN STREET

Despite its name, "Main" Street was not the first business district in East Toledo. The earliest commercial enterprises on the East Side began in the late 1840s along Front Street, which at that time skirted the river. Then in 1853, Oak Street and Euclid (originally called Cherry Street) were laid out, and the first bustling business district developed around that location.

Not until the late 1860s was the area now known as Main Street even platted. Before that it was still virgin timber and farm land with only a few scattered farmhouses such as the one still standing at 411 Platt Street. Also, at Front and Main there was a high hump-backed mound, and a large ravine, or swale, cut through the area where the Foodtown Plaza is today.

This irregular ground was leveled and graded in the early 1870s by Louis Montville, an East Side contractor, and the new street was finally ready to be developed. However, it would not be known by the name "Main Street" for many years to come.

"Sometime before 1875," writes Lawrence Davis who as Clerk of City Council during the 1930s published a history of Main Street, "the city of Toledo bought from the Toledo Bridge Co. a strip of land 50 feet wide, extending from Front Street to the first stone pier in the bridge, which was named Bridge Street." By 1881, this strip of land was widened to over 80 feet.

Meanwhile, by 1873, the portion of Main Street from Front to Starr Avenue, also called Bridge Street, was opened to a width of 60 feet and was macadamized in 1879. The continuation of the street across Starr Avenue to Greenwood was not laid out until 1895, and the section from Greenwood to Nevada waited until 1909.

Another extension of the street that ran from Nevada to Navarre Avenue existed as early as 1880, and was called South Bridge Street. That name was changed to Berry Street in 1918.

The name "Main Street" finally appeared in 1894. By then the street had become the East Side's main business section, running from Front Street to Starr Avenue, and merchants wanted the name of the street to reflect its prominence.

Many improvements to the street have been made over the years. On December 13, 1909, Council passed an ordinance requiring eighteen "whiteway" lights to be installed between Front and Second Street. Five years later the lights were extended to Starr Avenue. In 1912, Main Street was paved with sheet asphalt and the section from Front to the bridge was repaved with 3 and 1/2 inches of creosote wood block. The viaduct over the Pennsylvania railroad tracks was constructed in 1927.

Then in 1929 and 1930, through an extraordinary engineering feat, Main Street was widened from 60 to 75 feet by moving back all the buildings on the south side of the street. This remarkable accomplishment was achieved without damage to a single building, and it remains one of the best remembered events in the history of the East Side.

Many changes have taken place over the years. The old streetcar tracks on Main Street disappeared soon after the last car ran in 1939. Also, many older businesses gave way to newer ones.

By the 1950's Murphy's Department Store occupied
the Weber Block and J. C. Penney's was in the
Friedman Block at First & Main. Then the 1874
Garbe/Plumey Block (now Wendy's) and the Platt
Building (now McDonald's) both disappeared. The
1970s saw the building of the Foodtown Plaza, and
also the loss of the Montville Block and the Arlington
Hotel, both dating from the early 1890s.

But now there are encouraging signs of new
life all along Main Street. A revitalized Weber Block
again anchors the street at Front and Main, and new
businesses are joining older ones in many of the
familiar buildings. More changes will surely come,
but one thing remains the same. Even though there
are fine businesses throughout the East Side, Main
Street has been East Toledo's "main" street for
nearly a hundred years.

Widening Main Street, 1929.

THE MAN WHO OPENED MAIN STREET

The first roads on the East Side were the River Road, which later became Miami and Front Streets, and the Woodville Plank Road, an old Indian trail. Oak Street was surveyed in 1853, and that same year Cherry Street (Euclid) was opened but not turnpiked. Except for these roads and three early plats dating from the 1850s, East Toledo was still just open farm land and forest.

The man who opened Main Street was a contractor named Louis Montville. He also did the grading for many other streets in East Toledo that were surveyed before the turn of the century. Mr. Montville was born in 1837, and came to Toledo from his home in Watertown, New York, at the end of the Civil War.

He timed his move to Toledo very well. The first Cherry Street Bridge had just been built, and the East Side was only beginning its period of real growth. Gradually more and more farms were being divided into residential plats, and Mr. Montville was kept steadily employed.

Although he had little formal education, it was said that Mr. Montville had a genius for calculating the materials needed to do a job. He could tell at a glance, for example, the amount and value of the timber required to build a house. His associates remembered him to be "energetic" and "industrious," and he was a "highly esteemed" member of the East Side community during the forty years he was in the contracting business.

Main Street, at first called Bridge Street, was not opened until 1873. At that time, Mr. Montville used the fill from leveling the high bluff at Front and Main to raise the levels of Euclid, First, and Second Streets. The shallow ravine that ran through the area, a continuation of what is now Hecky's Pond, Ravine Park, and the Waite bowl, can still be seen around Euclid and First Street and the Foodtown Plaza. Although it became the East Side's most prestigious business address as early as 1877, it did not receive the name Main Street until 1894.

Mr. Montville's business continued to prosper as the East Side grew. He lived in the house that still stands at 440 First Street and owned more property in East Toledo at that time than anyone except Harvey Platt. His Montville Block stood at the northeast corner of First and Main where Barrett's Shoe Store was located for so many years. Built in the 1890s, the Montville Block remained an East Side landmark until it burned in 1975.

Mr. Montville's first wife, Liocadie, died in childbirth in 1874, the year after Main Street was opened. The baby, Honorah, died three days later, and was buried with her mother. The Montvilles also had three sons: Fred, Louis, Jr., and George; and daughters Adeline and Emma. Lizzie was born in 1881, after Mr. Montville had remarried. Like most East Siders of French descent, he was a member of St. Louis parish.

He continued to work until the day of his death. Returning from the Barbour & Starr Lumber Yard on May 27, 1907, he suffered a stroke and collapsed on the floor of the Summit and Broadway streetcar. Although his name is not as well known today as that of other prominent Toledoans, Louis Montville played a very important role in the early development and growth of the East Side.

HOW EAST SIDE STREETS GOT THEIR NAMES

Inhabitants west of the river who venture to the East Side, usually in search of Tony Packo's, often complain about getting lost in a tangle of streets. East Siders, however, seem to take pride in their knowledge of every street and are generally curious about how the streets got their names.

Most people are aware that Navarre Avenue was named for Peter Navarre and his brothers who in 1807 became the first settlers east of the river and who also served bravely as scouts for General William Henry Harrison during the War of 1812. But there are many other important pioneer settlers and outstanding citizens of East Toledo who would be forgotten today except for the East Side streets named in their honor.

Kelsey Avenue and Starr Avenue were named for families involved in the East Side's prosperous lumber business, which was begun when most of the land was still virgin forest. Alonzo Chesbrough, another lumberman, was probably East Toledo's first millionaire, and once had a beautiful mansion on the street that still bears his name.

James Raymer, commemorated by a street and school, was an early East Side real estate dealer and also a postmaster and member of the school board. His home was on the site later occupied by the Little Sisters of the Poor and is now Spring Grove Park on Starr Avenue. Howland Street is named for the Civil War era family who farmed that area, one member of which, Rev. Ezra Howland, started the first church on the East Side in 1849.

Rev. Howland's church was on Grand Avenue, subsequently changed to Consaul Street in honor of the family who had a large farm on that street out near Wheeling. Frank Consaul, grandson of the first Consauls who came to the area in the 1830s, later became a Toledo Councilman and lived at the corner of Euclid and Greenwood.

Fassett, Potter, Valentine, Paine, and Millard also were named for families who farmed in those areas. A member of the latter family, I. I. Millard, became a Probate Judge in Toledo, and his son Ralph was a president of the East Toledo Club. Dawson Street is named for Rev. Samuel Dawson, who started the Chapel at Oak and Hathaway in 1873 and also Second Baptist at Fourth and Steadman in 1864.

Charles O'Shea, a fireman at the former #13 Engine House, suggested that the street running past the high school should be changed from Gardner Street to Morrison Drive in honor of the former Chief Justice of the Supreme Court from Maumee, Morrison R. Waite, for whom the school is named. Mott Street, also in that area, was named for Richard Mott, a prominent Toledo pioneer and important early mayor of the city.

Hurd Street got its name from Frank Hurd, a congressman, free trader, and prominent public speaker. Dr. Harrison Hathaway, a physician and member of the library board, gave his name to the street located near his practice, which was formerly called Fort Street. Earl Street, according to one source, got its name from Erle Hamiliton, a former city alderman. Craig Street is named after Capt. John Craig, founder of the Craig Shipyards which later became American Shipbuilding.

In the days of the "wild frontier," western

names held a strange fascination for those back east. Such names that were once considered exotic are represented by East Toledo streets called Utah, Idaho (which was formerly Waite Street), Colorado, Denver, and Nevada (with its distinctive local pronunciation).

A large rolling mill once stood on Front Street where the Edison Acme Plant is today, and Steel and Carbon Streets were given their names during that era. At the opposite extreme from heavy industry, Walden Avenue is named after the pond where Henry David Thoreau retreated to write his famous book of that title. Arden Place is named for famous forests in France and Warwickshire, England.

Mason Street is named for James Mason, another early lumberman who lived in that area. Stillman Court recalls the Browns, Stillman and Daniel, who owned the large stockyards where the Weiler Homes now stands, and who also built the mansions on Miami Street in 1870 on the site that is now the Jobst Institute. Forsythe Street used to be called Brown Street.

Rogers Street got its name from the family of that name, one member of which was Alonzo Rogers who taught a private school near Oak and First Streets in 1852 and later served nineteen years on the Board of Education. Prentice Street is named in honor of the first white child born in Toledo, Frederick Prentice, who was another East Side millionaire and one of the donors of land for Prentice Park in 1858.

Over the years, the names of several East Side streets were changed. French Street, where the first immigrants from that country settled, later became Greenwood. Valleywood was once called Nasby Street, named for David Ross Locke's popular Civil War comic character, Petrolium V. Nasby. A partial list of other streets that once had different names is as follows:

Former Name	Current Name
Cherry	Euclid
Bridge	Main
Fort	Hathaway
Williams	Milton
Elm	Steadman
McCloud	Wheeling
Longfellow	York
Baker	Elmore
Grand	Consaul
Waite	Idaho
Big Ditch	Stadium

Even an East Sider could get lost on the streets in those days. But it is fortunate that the familiar street names of today still preserve some of the history east of the river which otherwise might have been completely forgotten.

BIRMINGHAM'S EARLY HISTORY

A librarian at Birmingham branch library, Betty Lee, compiled a history of the Birmingham area for Toledo's centennial celebration of 1937. An article by George Pearson has preserved many of the details of Miss Lee's research.

In 1890 John Manning opened the National Malleable Castings Company along the river on Front Street just north of Grand (now Consaul Street). Word of the good wages reached the old world and many Hungarian immigrants soon arrived in the area. Started with 200 men, the Malleable employed 1600 workers by the time of the first World War.

At that time the streetcar line went out Front Street only as far as the old Rolling Mill near the corner of East Broadway. But when the Malleable opened, the line was extended to Paine Avenue and later all the way out to Ironville.

Also in 1890 the National Milling Company was established by David Anderson, and other heavy industry in the area soon followed. The Toledo Furnace Company (later Interlake Iron) was started in 1902. Trotter Lumber Company was formed in 1903. And Craig Shipbuilding, which became the Toledo Shipbuilding Company in 1906, also located nearby. The area was named Birmingham because of its resemblance to the heavy iron and steel producing region of Birmingham, England.

Among other early businesses were John Nagy's coal yard started in 1895, the May Coal Company (1916), and the People's Dairy (1924). Some of the first Hungarians to settle in Birmingham were Charles and Louis Zettner, Mr. Nagy, Michael Csizmar, Andrew Toth, William Meyer, Stephen Molnar, Gabriel Bertok, John Strick, John Urban, Julius Simon, and Stephen Juhasz among others.

Originally, the whole area that became Birmingham consisted only of the Collins, Benedict, and Valentine farms. Judge J. F. Collins donated thirty acres of his farm to the city on the condition that the rest would be purchased for a park. Collins Park became one of the first in the city park system put together by Sylvanus Jermain in the late 1880's. The Valentine farm stood about where the Hungarian Reform Church is now located, and the Benedict farm was out Consaul street on land later occupied by brick yards.

Before the large Hungarian immigration of the 1890's, German and French settlers from Alsace-Lorraine lived in the area. Some of the prominent family names were Humphrey, Etau, Navarre, Holmes,

Valentine, and Reid. The first little red brick school
was across a creek on Wheeling Street. In 1892 a
four-room Birmingham School was built on the
location of the present school, which was enlarged
to 26 rooms in 1928. Samuel Howland was the first
principal and John Etau, former manager of the
Collins farm, was the first custodian.

Industry Along North Front Street.

Organized in 1920, the Birmingham library was
built in 1925. Some of the first librarians were
Eleanor Boyd, Catherine Gorman, Mrs. Albert Bihn,
and Margaret McCarthy.

The first church, Birmingham Congregational,

was established in 1892 on Paine Avenue near
Genesee Street. St. Stephen's, the first church for
the Hungarian residents, opened on January 1, 1899,
as did the school. The original frame building
burned down in 1908. The present beautiful church
complex dates from the 1920s. The Hungarian
Reformed Church was erected in 1903, St. Michael's
in 1915, and Holy Rosary (organized as St. Ignatius)
in 1913.

Although the Malleable, Paragon Oil, the brick
yards, and even Ironville are now all gone,
Birmingham remains one of Toledo's strongest ethnic
neighborhoods. Tony Packo's has received national
attention, the Birmingham festival attracts thousands
of people every year, and the Hungarian roots of the
community still nourish its residents. Birmingham's
strengths mentioned in Miss Lee's centennial history
are still, 56 years later, alive and well today.

OIL BOOM DAYS IN EARLY EAST TOLEDO

About the turn of the century, the famous
Klondike well came in on the Miller farm near Millard
Avenue in Ironville. This enormous gusher, which
was still producing oil forty years later, led to
feverish activity by drillers who took up leases and
soon had the area south and east of the city all
punctured full of holes. The automobile age was
beginning, and East Toledo was ready to provide the
fuel.

Already the discovery of oil in Wood County
had become a stabilizing force for Toledo during the
financial panic of 1893. Although not much oil was
ultimately found in Lucas County, it did not take
those early drillers to the south very long to realize
that the East Side was an ideal site for the refining

and shipping of oil and gasoline.

The first refineries on the East Side were Paragon Oil, located in Ironville between Front Street and the river; the Craig Oil Company, also in Ironville; and the Sun Company, formed under the leadership of Edward O. Emerson and Joseph N. Pew along Woodville Road in 1890. Later came Pure Oil, the Gulf Oil Company which had bought out Paragon, and the giant Standard Oil Company (now BP) which had been started by John D. Rockefeller. Frank Niles, an IRS collector and early resident along Bay Shore Road, told George Pearson that these companies came to East Toledo for the shipping advantages of the Great Lakes, which enabled them "to ship oil and gasoline to any port in the world."

But before the growth of the large refineries, the wells had to be brought in, and the "shooters" had the most dangerous job in the oil fields. After the well had been drilled, usually to a depth of about 1100 to 1200 feet in the oil producing Trenton rock, the "shooter" was called in. These daring men would then "shoot" the well with nitro-glycerine, which would often greatly increase the flow of the well. Shooters liked to gather at the Arlington Hotel, at the corner of Second and Main, and tell some of their hair-raising adventures to the proprietor, Joseph Munch, over a drink or two.

Because nitro-glycerine is such a volatile explosive, it was kept in caches out in the country as far as possible from any inhabitants. The shooter would bring the nitro to the well site in a buckboard or other light horse-drawn rig. Sometimes a tragedy would occur at the cache when the man was filling the cans or loading the explosive on the wagon. No one would ever know exactly what had happened, because the man and his team would be blown to bits, and only a deep hole would be left where the cache had been.

One such incident occurred out Starr Avenue near what is now the exit of Pearson Park. The explosion, as described in Josephine Fassett's <u>History of Oregon and Jerusalem Township</u>, shook houses for miles around, and all that was ever found were some remnants of the wagon and the unfortunate horse.

The Klondike Gusher, c. 1900

When the shooter arrived at the well, drillers and spectators would give him plenty of room. He would then fill a slender can with the explosive and carefully lower it to the bottom of the well. This would be followed by another can until there was enough nitro-glycerine in the well for the shoot. Measurements would be taken to make sure that the cans were in the right position.

Old-timers recalled thrilling tales of how the flow of oil would sometimes push the cans of explosive back to the top of the well. The shooter then had to catch them in his arms to save his life.

When all was ready, as George Pearson has described, someone would be "privileged" to drop the "Go-Devil" into the well to set off the charge. The "lucky" person would take the Go-Devil, a heavy piece of metal shaped appropriately like a bomb, drop it down the well, and "go like the devil!" A few moments later there would be a thud deep under the earth, then a shower of stones would clatter against the derrick, hopefully to be followed by an increased flow of oil.

George W. Barnes, Tom Wolf, R. G. Stitt, and the Shaffer brothers were some of the men who operated in the early East Toledo oil fields. In those days Mayor Samuel "Golden Rule" Jones and his son Percy could be seen in Ironville at their sucker-rod and oil supply plant. Also, Clarence and Nye Bingham were busy hauling boilers, derrick timbers, and other supplies into the oil fields, often through a sea of mud.

Even though the oil in this area proved "spotty," the hard work of these men has had a lasting effect on the economy east of the river. The large refineries that grew out of those early boom years recall the excitement and danger faced by the pioneer drillers, haulers, and shooters who brought the oil industry to the East Side when the automobile was young.

A GLIMPSE OF EAST TOLEDO IN THE YEAR 1900

When Toledo celebrated its centennial in 1937, reporter George Pearson provided a glimpse of what living on the East Side was like thirty-seven years earlier at the very beginning of the 20th Century.

In 1900, long before modern construction tie-ups on the Craig Bridge, traffic was often reduced to "a snail's pace" on the old Cherry Street Bridge, because there was not enough clearance for streetcars and two lanes of traffic at the same time. Everyone went at the pace of the slowest horse that happened to be crossing the river at that moment.

Main Street from Front to Starr Avenue had only a single streetcar track, so coaches had to wait at the switches for a streetcar coming in the opposite direction to pass. Front Street was not paved past Dearborn, and the streetcars going to Ironville often "went bobbing along, sometimes in a sea of mud, for the street at times was almost impassible." There were no train viaducts either, so railroad watchmen had to be on duty at the grade crossings both at the Pennsylvania tracks on Main Street and the New York Central crossing on East Broadway.

Most of East Toledo's churches and schools existed at that time, but few of them in their current buildings. Both Sacred Heart (under Father Eilert) and Good Shepherd (Father O'Brien) were built in the year 1900 to replace wooden structures. The only other church buildings that have survived since the turn of the century are the Dawson Chapel (1873) at Oak and Hathaway, the old Second Congregational (1894) on Fourth Street, and the first chapel of Martin Luther (1892) at Nevada and Arden.

The only school building still in use from 1900 is Sacred Heart School (1889, remodeled 1954). Most of the original grade school buildings were replaced in the 1920s, with East Side Central the last to be replaced in 1960. Waite was not built until 1913.

Businesses along Main Street in 1900 included L. E. Flory's dry goods store in the Weber Block at Front and Main, and the Cook Brothers drug store across the street. Beside the Weber Block in a little building still standing was the East Side Bank, and the Herman and Gross grocery was next door at First and Main. Herman and Gross built the large block that later became Finkbeiner's Furniture (Carty's grandfather) and then J. C. Penney's.

Across First Street in the Montville Block was the hardware store of M. V. Wolf, who later became the first president of the Commercial Savings Bank and built the large home at Arden and Greenwood. Bearded Joseph Gschwind had his harness shop nearby, and Chris Rantz had a barber shop at Second and Main across from Joseph Munch's Arlington Hotel.

On the other side of Main Street between First and Second was the drug store of David Harpster, the father of D. Harry Harpster. W. T. Davies had opened a grocery store at Sixth and Main next to Gus Eberlin's meat market, and the Davies Building is still standing, as is the Harpster Block. Two pioneer businesses on Starr Avenue were W. J. VonEwegen's drug store and E. J. Smith's grocery.

Dr. Seth Beckwith had a coroner's office on Main Street near Second, and also his own office next to his home at Main and Starr. Dr. J. D. Ely's office was in Southeast Toledo (the Miami-Fassett area), and with the leadership of Dr. Clarence Ordway the East Side Hospital was developed in that area.   George Parks and Richard Clegg had established undertaking businesses, and Hoeflinger's funeral home at Platt and Second was built in the year 1900.

Henry and Amos Crane, along with J. D. Chamberlin, had farms out Miami Street toward where Captain Ford was just bringing his plate-glass business to what is now Rossford. The Cranes were market gardeners who pioneered the shipment of lettuce, and Mr. Chamberlin is credited as being "an originator of the idea of preserving fruit in hermetically sealed cans."   The Smith Bridge Company was also in that area, as was the construction company of Joseph Jackson, whose son William became Mayor of Toledo thirty years later.

East Toledo experienced its greatest growth between the 1880s and the 1920s, and these memories of George Pearson from the turn of the century help capture the importance of that year in the midst of the East Side's early development.

Chapter 5

SHOPPING DAYS...

*

Some East Side Businesses

from

The Weber Block

to

E. J. Smith's Food Fair

*

THE WEBER BLOCK: CORNERSTONE OF BUSINESS DISTRICT

Now a flourishing anchor of the East Side business community, the Weber Block narrowly escaped the wrecking-ball to reach its centennial in 1988. Today it is an exciting redevelopment success story.

The Weber Block, which stands on the corner of Front & Main, is perhaps more familiar to East Siders as the old Murphy's Department Store. A few may remember when it was Morris's five-and-dime or even Liggett's Rexall Drugs. For most of the

1980s, however, it was occupied only by the "Lady Ghost" who is said to have roamed its once lavish rooms and hallways.

The three-story brick Queen Anne structure was built on the East Side as an investment by John and Gustave Weber, clothing merchants downtown on Monroe Street. Their primary tenant was L. E. Flory, who had started his dry goods and clothing business in the Platt Building across the street in 1885.

Mr. Flory was a business partner with B. R. Baker, and they moved into the Weber Block together when it opened, occupying the prominent corner location. Mr. Baker soon moved across the river to Summit Street in 1894, but L. E. Flory and Company remained in the Weber Block for many more years, and in business on Main Street for over 50 years. A member of the Elks' crack drill-team called the Cherry Pickers, he still walked to work every day when he was nearly 80.

The East Side Business College, under the leadership of Melvin Severance who later taught business courses at Waite High School, opened its doors in September 1895. An advertisement in the city directory of that year lists "A Splendid Library," "Banking and Office Training," and "Actual Business Practice from the Beginning" among the attractions for students.

Although the school left the Weber Block after only five years, traces of its existence remained up until the renovations of last year. An "Office" sign still could be seen in faint lettering on the second floor wall above the old school's closed off Front Street entrance. Other long-forgotten occupants of those early years include a post office, an A & P store, and the Odd Fellows Corn City Lodge.

In the 1890s the large Alvin Theater, opening

on Front Street, was added to the back of the building. Its high-peaked roof, shown in early photographs, was removed after being damaged by the Maumee Chemical explosion in 1962. The theater, with its 24-foot high ceiling, could hold up to 300 people when well-known Vaudeville acts played in Toledo. The coatroom, ticket window, tin ceilings, balcony, and hand-carved wooden railings can still be seen nearly fifty years after they were last used by any paying customers.

The confusing labyrinth of rooms on the second floor was once the Columbia Hotel. Opened in 1918, it provided rooms for the tide of immigrants who were arriving to fill the new jobs in East Toledo's rapidly expanding industries. Many Bulgarian immigrants settled in the Front & Main area, and a Bulgarian athletic club operated on the third floor as late as the 1930s. Eastern European writing found on the wide central stairway leading to the third floor has been preserved. The mysterious message in the strange alphabet has been deciphered to read merely "Watch Your Step."

Many railroad workers also occupied rooms in the old hotel. But during the Depression the hotel declined and was finally closed by the Board of Health in 1932. There are stories of a murder being committed in those long-deserted rooms, but no concrete evidence for that has been found. Peeling wallpaper did reveal a plasterer's signature of 1896.

Union meetings were held on the third floor. Over the stage in the old union hall can still be seen the "Industrial Workers of the World" mural. But no meetings have been held there since the volatile labor days of the 1930s.

The best known occupant of the third floor was the prominent athletic club of the teens and 1920s. The former gymnasium still has its beautiful wood-beam ceiling and a wooden roller that was used to lower a dividing curtain during boxing matches. A faded sign still remainds long expired members that dues were one dollar per month.

There are also the remains of a primitive two-story shower stall. An attendant would climb the stairs over the shower area and pour buckets of water on the sweaty athlete below.

Many boxing matches were held in the old gym. It is said that Jess Willard trained there for his famous title bout with Jack Dempsey held in Toledo at Bay View Park on July 4th, 1919, but no newspaper account has been found to verify the story (or to show that Willard trained much at all). Dempsey won the fight and the title, and went on to become the dominant fighter of the Roaring 20s.

The Weber Block in 1896.

During the depths of the Depression, no new business tenants could be found for the upper stories of the building, so they remained vacant for over fifty years. Liggett's Drug Store occupied the first floor corner location during the 1920s and 30s, followed by Morris's Five & Dime during the 1940s. In March 1955, G. C. Murphy's opened using the whole first floor and part of the basement.

But when Murphy's closed in the late 1970s, the building's countdown toward demolition began. The problem of vandalism and water streaming through the roof caused the owners to think of tearing it down. Through the efforts of Jeff Eversman and the East Toledo Historical Society and Don Monroe of the River East Revitalization Corporation an attempt to save the building was launched.

In 1986 tours were arranged, and hundreds of people for the first time in a couple generations saw the whole building. Community interest in saving the building continued to grow, and River East was able to purchase it and prevent its demolition. A 100th birthday party was held in December 1988 as the first floor was still being renovated.

Today several businesses occupy the first floor, and the East Toledo Historical Society has several museum cases in the large concourse area. The University of Toledo has business incubators on the second floor, which has been restored to resemble its originial Victorian appearance. The "Lady Ghost" now has more company than she has had in many years, and the East Side again has a cornerstone for its business community.

EAST SIDE BUSINESSES KEPT ALL IN THE FAMILY

"Like father, like son" held true for many well-known East Side businesses, and many times it was "like daughter" as well. A surprisingly large number of sons and daughters followed in the footsteps of their parents, taking over established businesses and keeping them in the family for several generations.

Dr. Seth Beckwith began practicing on the East Side in the 1880s, originally on First Street, then on Main near Second Street. Later he settled at Starr & Main where the large red-brick house he built in the early 1890s still stands. Dr. Beckwith introduced the first X-ray machine in East Toledo, one of the first in the city.

Some attributed his death to demonstrating the new technique too frequently when the dangerous effects of over-exposure to X-rays were still not well understood. His son, Horace K. Beckwith, carried on the practice, with less use of X-rays, for many years in the same office at Starr & Main.

R. S. Clegg opened an undertaking business on Starr Avenue near Platt Street in 1895, the same year the fire station was built at Starr & Main. A skilled cabinet-maker, he was known for the coffins he made, including his own. He later developed a thriving ambulance business as well. Clegg's sons, James and Worth, carried on the funeral and ambulance business, each with his own establishment.

The first funeral director on the East Side was Michael Hoeflinger, who started in business on Main Street about 1880. A funeral home was built at Second and Platt in 1900 where the old horse stalls that were used in the early years of the century can still be seen. A few years ago the business moved to a new location on Navarre near Coy in Oregon. Michael Hoeflinger's son, Theodore, who recently died at the age of 94, spent his life in the business, and it has continued to remain in the family now for well over 100 years.

David Harpster arrived on the East Side from Carey, Ohio, in 1888. He built the brick block at 136 and 138 Main Street and began operating a drug store and wallpaper store. He also served as president of the Commercial Savings Bank and Trust Company, which was organized on the East Side. His son, D. Harry Harpster, continued to run the wallpaper store for many years.

W. F. Barrett moved to East Toledo in 1899 from Alpena, Michigan, and opened a shoe store at 302 Main Street. Four years later he moved the store to 135 Main Street in the Montville Block, where his sons Lawrence and Tyler Barrett along with Mrs. Barrett maintained the family business for many years. Barrett's Shoe Store remained a well-known business on the East Side for over 70 years until the building burned down in 1975.

There were many other businesses that passed down through East Side families for generations. One of the earliest was the coal company started by Alex Forster, who came to Toledo in 1872. He first worked at the old stockyards where the Weiler Homes now stand. He then started a coal business at Oak and Earl Streets which was continued by his son Frank for many more years.

William J. VonEwegen opened a drug store at Starr and East Broadway in 1892. The business was

carried on at the same location until only recently
by his son Herbert VonEwegen. Also, William Garbe's
hardware store on Euclid Avenue was passed on to
his sons Harry and Arthur.

The business of S. A. Save (a great name for
a department store) was carried on for many years
by his son Leon Save. In addition, E. J. Smith,
Herman Gross, Johlin's Winery, and the Toppins of
the East Side Sun also had sons and daughters who
continued family businesses on the East Side.

One of the longest family run businesses in
the country was L. A. Metzger's dry goods and
groceries. Started at Front & Main during the
presidency of Zachary Taylor, the business remained
in the family for 117 years until the 1960s.

Perhaps the most unusual example of a father-
son transition was not in a business, but in a school.
Henry VanGorder became principal of Franklin
School in the late 1930s, the same school his father,
R. C. VanGorder, had served as principal for over
forty years. Together they were principals of
Franklin School for 64 years.

These are only some examples that show the
strong family ties on the East Side. One of the
reasons East Toledo has traditionally been a stable
community is that many businesses have survived
for such a long time by keeping them for
generations all in the family.

TAILOR RECALLS EARLY DAYS IN EAST TOLEDO

Henry C. Thibodeau, early East Side tailor,
was in business on Main Street for nearly fifty
years. His memories of East Toledo, recorded by

George Pearson, give a glimpse of what life was like on the East Side during the early years of the 20th century.

Born in Michigan, Mr. Thibodeau attended school at Chatham, Ontario, and first worked in the tailoring business in Windsor. He remembered as a young man visiting the grave of the runaway slave that Harriet Beecher Stowe used as a model in Uncle Tom's Cabin. The cemetery was in Dresden, Ontario, a northern terminus of the Underground Railroad.

While he was still working as a cutter at a tailor shop in Windsor, Mr. Thibodeau happened to visit Milan, Michigan. There he noticed what seemed like large crowds of people downtown on a Saturday, which led him to believe that Milan would be a good place to open his own business. So he went into partnership with a Detroit tailor, also of French origin, named Frank Desmarais, and together they started a shop.

They soon discovered, however, that only a few of the men in those "large crowds" of Milan could afford tailor-made suits. Some of the men even wore their overalls downtown on Sundays, Mr. Thibodeau recalled, which was not an encouraging sign for his business.

Then one day he met a lumberman, Jerome Trembley, who lived on East Broadway in the French section of East Toledo. Mr. Trembley told him of the advantages found on the East Side, and in the early 1890s Mr. Thibodeau decided to locate in that booming community east of the Maumee River.

He then made his first visit to Toledo where he met L. A. Metzger, who also encouraged him to do business on the East Side. He opened his first shop in the Weber Block, but a few weeks later bought the shop at 144 Main Street where he remained for 46 years. That shop was formerly owned by another

tailor, Martin Smith, who was the father of East Side
grocer E. J. Smith.

At that time, Mr. Thibodeau recalled, Main
Street and Cherry (Euclid) were the only streets
that were paved. By that, he meant "paved" with
cobblestones. Some of his business neighbors on
Main Street were hardware dealers Wolf & Keller,
grocers Henry & Gross who soon built the Friedman
Block (later the J. C. Penney store), and Baker &
Flory in the Weber Block.

Mr. Thibodeau became an active member of St.
Louis Parish, the church most East Siders of French
lineage attended. Many other French families had
settled in East Toledo by the turn of the century,
primarily in the area around East Broadway and
Greenwood, which was at that time called French
Street.

Proud of his heritage, Mr. Thibodeau
organized the first French Day in Toledo, and was
its first president. In the years just before World
War I, it was an annual occasion, first held at White
City out Auburn Avenue and later at Navarre Park.
As many as 12,000 French people would attend the
event, coming from as far away as Montreal.

The tailoring business proved to be
prosperous for Mr. Thibodeau. There were many
successful businessmen living on the East Side who
could afford the distinction of wearing tailor-made
clothing. Mr. Thibodeau liked to recall the days
when creased trousers were evidence that a suit was
not made by a tailor. But to give the impression
their clothes were more costly, men would often come
into his shop just to have the creases pressed out
of their pants.

For many years Mr. Thibodeau boarded at
Munch's Hotel, first at Front and Main where
McDonald's is today. Joseph Munch then built the

Hotel Arlington at Main and Second Street. Mr. Thibodeau remembered the kindness of the Munch family, and spoke in the highest terms of Mrs. Munch, who once nursed him through a severe illness.

He survived that illness to become a well-known fixture on Main Street. Many establishments stayed in business a long time in those days, but few lasted longer than the tailor shop of this French-Canadian who decided to settle in East Toledo nearly a century ago.

THE LAST DAYS OF PEERLESS LAUNDRY

The old Peerless Laundry building, a familiar sight to East Siders for a century, has finally bitten the dust. Last May, the facade crumbled into the street at the corner of Front and Oak, leaving the interior exposed. Now the rest of the building has been torn down almost exactly one hundred years after it was first occupied.

Peerless Laundry was founded by George Ryan in 1889, and he moved into the building at 402 Front Street three years later. In early photographs, a young Mr. Ryan with curling handlebar mustache confidently reflects the prosperity found in East Toledo during those last years of the 19th century.

In 1897, a booklet called "Toledo: An Ohio Gem" describes Peerless as "one of the foremost laundries" in the "cleanly city of Toledo." The 20 by 80 foot building was "devoted entirely to the laundry business," and Mr. Ryan lived down the street at 402 Oak. In its prime, the company employed twenty people.

A 30-horse boiler and 10-horse engine
provided the power to run the latest machinery.
Special attention was given to commercial and hotel
volume, and Mr. Ryan owned several wagons to
receive and deliver goods. He even drilled a private
artesian well on the premises to insure a continuous
supply of pure, clean water for the laundry.

Peerless Laundry Building, 1989.

Mr. Ryan was a Toledo native and was
involved in several local clubs and civic
organizations. He also seems to have gained the
respect of the business community. An early
publication said of his work that "it is hazarding
nothing to say no better laundry work is done
within the confines of the State."

In spite of this praise by Mr. Ryan's contemporaries, it is difficult to judge how well the business prospered as the 20th century approached. In any event, by 1909 the business had closed and Mr. Ryan had left town.

Over the next few years, the building housed a succession of of grocery stores and small restaurants that served the Bulgarian immigrants moving into the Front Street area. In 1917, for example, Evanoff's Grocery, which was also a pool hall and restaurant, was located there. Draganoff's Shoe Repair was there in 1928, and by 1932 the building was the Helen Popoff Restaurant.

From 1934 to the 1950s Tomlin Corporation, a company that dealt in oil equipment, used the building, followed by Young Gas Station Equipment which was there until about 1981. For the last ten years the building had been vacant.

Despite the fact that it was occupied by all these businesses over the years, the building still retained the old Peerless Laundry sign that ran the length of the roofline along the side of the structure. This faded old sign painted high on the brick wall was a reminder of a business that once prospered on the East Side, even though that business had been gone for over 80 years. Now the building and the old Peerless sign are only memories as well.

OHIO BRICKS: AS TOUGH AS THE MEN WHO MADE THEM

Although not as famous as the old brickyard in Indianapolis that later became a racetrack, the Ohio Brick Company, once located on Consaul Street between Paine Avenue and the Toledo Terminal

Railroad Tracks, is still remembered by many long-time East Side residents. Even though the last brick with the distinctive "Ohio" stamped on it was produced forty years ago, a large number of those bricks still remain in houses all around Toledo.

Ohio Brick began operations at the Consaul Street yard in 1902, with main offices downtown in the Spitzer Building. The first officers of the company were A. Kuhlman, President; George Metzger, Vice-President; and Richard Kind, Secretary. The company was long associated with the Kuhlmans, and later with the William F. DeSana family on the East Side.

In the 1920s, the downtown offices were moved to the Nicholas Building, but the yard remained at the Consaul Street location until the company closed in the late 1940s. All existing accounts testify to the high quality of the bricks that were made here in East Toledo. A Cleveland publication of 1929 mentions only the Collinwood Company and Ohio Brick Company as producing bricks free from polluting calcium salts that weakened the strength of the bricks.

Making the best possible bricks was as much of an art as a science. The brickmaker's art consisted of knowing just how long to bake the bricks in the kiln. An experienced brickmaker looking through the peep-hole of the oven could tell by the color of the brick when it was done. The temperature was controlled by changing the flow of air into the oven.

If the brick was not baked long enough, it would be too weak and had to be thrown away. An "overcooked" brick, called a "clinker," would not fit well with other bricks and was kept in separate piles. These overbaked bricks, often "as hard as steel," would be sold in batches for special building projects. Occasionally a whole house would be built entirely with clinkers. A good brickmaker such as William Giles, who was yard manager in the 1930s and 40s, had to know how to mix the raw materials that went into the molds and also how to run the huge machinery that operated the presses.

Working at the brickyard was certainly not an easy job. The author's father, Richard Michaels, who worked for Ohio Brick from 1938 to 1941, recalled some of his experiences at the Consaul Street yard. Before the days of pallets and fork-lifts, bricks had to be loaded and unloaded from trucks and trains entirely by hand.

Ohio Brick Company about 1940.

Men wearing rubber-coated gloves would "toss" the bricks six at a time. The first man would grab six bricks, turn them vertically, and toss them up to the catcher who would then pluck them out of the air, turn them back horizontally, and put them in the truck or boxcar. Several hours of this activity eliminated any need for a health club membership.

Mr. Michaels also had the job of paymaster. Since the workers were always paid in cash, he would take a taxi downtown to the Nicholas Building twice a month (with a gun in his pocket) to pick up the money. When he returned to the yard, he would put the money in separate envelopes for each worker.

Sometimes when there was an over-supply of bricks, the yard would be shut down. During those times many of the men would ask for the job of night watchman to make a little extra money. Brickworkers were hardy individuals who could not afford to miss a paycheck, so when one would catch a bad cold the remedy was to simply drink a little kerosene.

After the yard closed, the quarry from which the clay was dug became a city dump. Today, instead of a racetrack, a trailer park sits on the site of the landfill.

Although not as well known as oil refining or shipbuilding, brickmaking has been an important industry on the East Side. Nothing remains of the many buildings at the Consaul Street yard, but evidence of the Ohio Brick Company can still be seen in the countless houses with a distinctive "Ohio" embedded in their bricks.

LAST REMAINS OF THE ANDES TIRE & RUBBER COMPANY

During the first years of the automobile industry, the East Side had its own tire company. The Andes Tire & Rubber Company disappeared long ago, but it has left behind its legacy in the names of two East Side streets platted about that time. According to East Toledo historian Cal O. Gettings, Goodyear Street, which runs south off Starr Avenue, and Goodrich Street, off Seaman Road, owe their names to this long-forgotten company.

The company was organized about the time of World War I, and a large structure was built out Starr Avenue near the terminal tracks where the expressway overpass is today. A foundation at least 150 feet square was laid, and a one-story building of reinforced concrete was constructed. The demand for tires was increasing rapidly at that time as more and more people were able to own automobiles.

Even though Toledo was in a convenient location for an auto-related business, Andes Tire & Rubber did not last long. The company soon went bankrupt and passed through a number of hands, including the Tower Company, until it was finally bought out by U. S. Tire.

The large building on Starr Avenue later became the East Side yard of the Hixon-Peterson Lumber Company. They added a wooden structure on top of the original concrete building in 1927. Hixon-Peterson used the building until 1932 when the Depression began to hurt the construction industry and the East Side yard was abandoned.

During the Depression, as New Deal programs were implemented in Toledo, the building was used as a barracks for the workers employed by the government for various building projects around the area. Local people remember attending dances held there, in which the building would swing to the music of the big bands of that era.

After the Second World War, the Cranes, who farmed land on Oregon Road, used the again abandoned building as a warehouse to store alfalfa meal. That arrangement, however, was soon cut short.

Mr. Gettings recalled driving along Dearborn Avenue with his family one Sunday afternoon in 1948, and noticing a wisp of smoke curling from the roof of the building. He knew it was going to be a huge fire and immediately headed for home. Soon all the roads were blocked, as every fire department on the East Side responded to the alarm.

The fire burned for over a week. A large stone chimney had been added when the building was a barracks, and every day Mr. Gettings' children would walk out Starr Avenue to see it still standing above the smouldering ruins. One day they arrived just in time to see the chimney collapse into the debris of what was once the Andes Tire & Rubber Company.

Years later Mr. Gettings found an old stock certificate from 1921 showing that his father owned fifteen shares in a company organized from the original Andes Tire & Rubber. Mr. Gettings' father should have no doubt purchased Goodyear or Goodrich stock, but at least that old certificate is proof that the once-important tire company did play a part in the history of the East Side, and perhaps influenced the naming of two of its streets.

OLD DIRECTORY ADVERTISES EAST SIDE IN 1906

What was it like to live in East Toledo in 1906? What kind of things did people need, and where did they go to get them? East Side historian Cal O. Gettings preserved an old directory whose ads give a glimpse of life in East Toledo nearly 90 years ago.

To do any serious courting, a young man would need to wear the latest fashions. For as little as $10 these "modern makes" could be purchased at Christian Textor's shop on Main Street, where he claimed "A Pretty Girl Goes With Nearly Every Suit," and then in fine print: "You Get the Suit Here--The Girl Afterwards."

Across the street at 130 Main, the Mahon Sisters sold women the latest millinery, reminding their fashion-conscious customers that they carried "the New York and Buffalo styles." Both men's and women's clothing was available at L. E. Flory's store in the Weber Block at Front and Main.

Next door to Textor's, shoes could be bought at W. F. Barrett's, the "Economy Shoe Store" that also offered brown, blue, and green trading stamps. Only two doors further up the street Bruot and Beucler were selling high fashion shoes "for tasteful particular people." It was obvious, however, which store East Siders preferred, as Bruot and Beucler soon disappeared while Barrett's would stay in business at the same location for another 70 years.

People were not the only creatures needing

shoes in those days. Mr. Gettings' father, Claud R.
Gettings, was already operating his "Blacksmithing
and Horse Shoeing" business at 2012 Starr Avenue.
But he certainly did not have a monopoly on the
trade.   Bercher   and   Werning,   who   also   built
carriages and wagons, had a blacksmith shop on
Main Street; Mr. C. M. Doan was located around the
corner on Front, where he paid "special attention to
interfering horses"; W. W. Murphy was at 951 Oak
Street; Mr. E. Kuhman had a shop in Ironville; and
J. B. Allen did blacksmithing at 141 Euclid beginning
in 1896 in a building that still bears his name
engraved in stone near the roof.

The rapid growth of the East Side at the turn
of the century is apparent in the number of building
supplies advertised in the directory.   The Toledo
Building Supply Company, "dealers in all kinds of
building material," was on Main at the foot of the
Cherry Street bridge.   Ohio Brick had its yard on
Consaul Street, and Northern Brick Company was at
Navarre and Thurston.   For wooden supplies there
was Washburn & Harris, Lumber Dealers, at the
corner of Oak and Earl Streets, and also the East
Side Lumber Company on Starr Avenue.   D. W.
DeVaux would paint or paper your home, and D.
Harry Harpster also had a wallpaper business at 138
Main Street.   At 211 Main was F. E. Walker, architect.

Many   businesses   of   1906   catered   to   the
stomachs of hungry East Siders.   The appropriately
named Munch Grocery at 135-7 Oak Street advertised
"lower prices than any other store in the city," and
E. J. Smith's Food Fair had already been in business
for 17 years on Starr Avenue.

Joseph Bordeau (926 Woodville), M. Bippus &
Son (301 Fassett), the Rodemich Brothers (1129
Miami), and C. R. Olds (Fassett & Utah) all operated
grocery stores at that time.   For those who wished
to dine out, Newingham's Restaurant near Front &
Main offered "Good Grub" at a cost of 15 cents a

meal. Poole's Hotel at Platt and Front had rooms for $1 per day and "regular meals" that cost 20 cents.

Thirst could also be quenched at a number of East Side establishments. Sam Trudeau's Pool Room and Bowling Alley at 195 Millard sold "wines, liquors, and tobaccos." J.C. McKindley thoughtfully provided "free accomodations for buggies and wagons" while his fine wines and liquors were being purchased. Jacob Lustig, "jobber of cigars," also dealt in "imported and domestic wines and whiskies." And there was always the Home Bottling Company at 418 Main Street.

For those who imbibed too freely, a trip to McGuire's Utah Pharmacy at 122 Fassett Street might be in order. William J. Von Ewegen, at Starr and East Broadway, was already selling prescription drugs in 1906. For 50 cents a customer could buy Tonic-Nervine, a "certain and safe cure" for such diverse illnesses as "fluttering of the heart" and "epilepsy." The only physician advertising in the directory was Clarence S. Ordway, in practice at 1153 Oak Street where he would soon open the East Side's first hospital. There were already, however, a "dog hospital" and two veterinarians.

In the end, if all else failed, there were five undertaking businesses in the directory, including the familiar names of Hoeflinger, Clegg, and Eggleston. George M. Parks advertised "the only automobile ambulance in the state of Ohio." Other morticians were Blanchard & Son at 431 East Broadway and O'Sullivan & Sullivan at 639 Oak. Undertakers also rented out their hacks for "parties, weddings, etc." Krueger Brothers' Florists, across Clark Street from Good Shepherd, could provide "choice cut flowers" for either the funerals or the weddings.

For those who are curious about what life was like for East Toledoans in 1906, these ads in Mr.

Gettings' give a fascinating hint of the tastes, fashions, habits, and daily routines of the people living east of the river nearly 90 years ago.

OLD ADVERTISEMENTS RECALL DEPRESSION YEARS

One of the intriguing aspects of owning a time-machine would be the bargains that today's inflated dollars could purchase at earlier prices. Examples of such rock-bottom prices were found on the back of a 1936 article from The Blade. These early ads not only recall the prices of the Depression era, but also are a reminder of the daily lives of Toledoans at that time.

Hudson's Furniture Company, in their ad, "challenges you to beat their low prices" and also "guarantees you the difference if at any time you can find a lower price in any store." Their 1936 prices would definitely be hard to beat today. For example, for just $39.50 you could purchase "group one," which included an English two-piece living room suite, walnut-finish end table, walnut-finish occasional table, chrome and black floor and table lamps, axminster throw rug, and silk pillow. No wonder they called themselves "Toledo's underselling furniture store."

Redd's Furniture Store at 504 Main Street was offering four full rooms of furniture for only $80. The Glowacki Furniture Company was selling electrical appliances for the home such as a Maytag washer "with round porcelain tub" for $59.50 (reduced $10), a four cubic-foot Frigidaire for $79.50, and a used model for $59.50. At these prices, ice boxes were still very much in use.

A 1936 Garland gas range also cost $59.50, but

a table top range was only $39.50. Terms as low as $3.65 a month were offered to installment buyers. If the laundry was really piling up, another ad offered to accept "any article in exchange for a good used $25 washer."

During the Depression, forty to eighty dollars was a large investment for many people. For that reason, appliances were kept for a long time, and Lane Electric at 418 Main Street could do a healthy business keeping those costly appliances in good repair. Buying used appliances was also popular. An ABC spinner washer "in A-1 condition" was offered for $18, and an "almost new" gas range was also advertised for the same price.

The Good Housekeeping Shop was giving away a free 1936 license plate with the purchase of a new Round Oak Gas Stove. They also admitted that "we may be foolish to sell these curley mohair living room suites for so little, but we are making a lot of friends and a little money."

There were also great savings on clothing in 1936. A shopper could go into the Starr Avenue Bargain House at 675 Platt Street and buy 100% wool Hart, Shaffner & Marks suits for $7.50. Their most expensive suits were $12.50. At Mickey's a topcoat sold for $9 and an all wool suit for $10. Miller's was selling Florsheim shoes for $3.50 a pair.

Some items seemed to be rather expensive for that time, while others cost even less than expected. An electric sweeper "running A-1" cost only $6, but an Eldredge sewing machine sold for $49.50 and up. A "like new" brown reed baby buggy was advertised for $10, but a new breakfast set with five-piece extension table was only $11.45. A person could buy a Voigtlander camera with "copar lens" and "double extension bellows" that used "film-pack, plates, or cut film" for $29.50. A "double coil tank heater," however, was only $3.75.

Among food items, dill pickles sold for 40 cents a gallon, sweet pickles for 95 cents. Hot peppers were 17 and a half cents per quart and horseradish was 30 cents a quart. Some of the more unusual items to appear in these ads were fine or coarse cinders ($3.50 per yard), cedar fence posts, a walk-in cooler, a ten-foot lunch counter, and a "used five-foot bathtub on legs complete with new faucets" for $15.

These old ads show that even though prices have changed, advertising remains much the same. If a time-machine could transport us back to 1936, we would find some terrific bargains, but (like today) also a lot of overpriced junk.

MEMORIES OF EAST SIDE CHRISTMAS SHOPPING

In a closely knit community like East Toledo, residents in the early days tended to shop in the nearby stores where they knew and trusted the merchants. This was especially true at Christmas time. May Schoonmaker has recorded her memories of Christmas shopping at her father's store in the early years of this century.

Her father, T. J. Torrence, had a store in the Commager Block at 132 Main Street. It was called the Handy Store because of the variety of items sold there. Among his goods were china crockery, silverware, tea and coffee pots, candy, spices, and toys, all of which were imported. With such gift items, Mr. Torrence did a large share of his business during the holidays.

Mrs. Schoonmaker recalled how the week before Christmas customers would be packed into the store elbow to elbow. One year a customer lost a twenty dollar bill, which was a lot of money then, but it could not be found in the crush of shoppers in the store. Only after closing time was the valuable bill found under the edge of a counter.

Mrs. Torrence used to do the Christmas decorating in her husband's store. She would dress up a large doll that had movable joints and display it in the front window. Along with the life-like doll would also be a doll buggy, cradle, and a small china cabinet that held children's play dishes.

In those early days Mr. Torrence made deliveries to his customers' homes. He hired a dray-mare to pull the delivery wagon, but often preferred to make his rounds on a bicycle. Many times he would carry a twelve-piece dinner setting of china in his bicycle basket over the bumpy roads far out into the country, perhaps as a testimony to the sturdiness of his wares.

At the turn of the century when many immigrants were moving into the East Side, it was necessary to have clerks who could speak other languages. Mr. Torrence always had two lady clerks, one who spoke French and the other German. For many years the French-speaking lady was Anna LeRoux. One of the Hoeflinger daughters served as the German clerk, a job later passed on to two of her cousins, Sophia and Bertha Keifer.

When the store was especially crowded, the clerk would be seated on a raised platform. This was also the custom, as many East Siders remember, at Barrett's Shoe Store across the street in the Montville Block. The platform not only showed the customers where to pay for their purchases, but it also helped the clerk keep an eye on everyone in the store.

During the Christmas season of 1939, some of the bargains that were available in nearby stores included tennis racquets for $1.39, wrist watches for $2.10, and a Western Flyer bicycle for $19.95 at Western Auto (408-10 Main Street). Lownsbury's at 425 Main had automobiles for sale for as little as $5 to $15 down.

Newer businesses have replaced such long-time merchants as Flory, Metzger, Redd, Plumey, Harpster, Barrett, and Torrence. The Commager Block still stands at First and Main, as does the Torrence home at 640 Parker, but the Handy Store is only a fading memory. Yet when the Christmas shopping season comes around, many East Siders, in spite of the modern suburban malls, still patronize the merchants on Main Street, just as their parents and grandparents did many Christmases ago.

THE HISTORY OF E.J. SMITH'S FOOD FAIR

Edward Joseph Smith, for many years East Toledo's best known grocer, opened his first store on Starr Avenue in 1889. Over the years, his dedication to the business was legendary. When an attack of influenza kept him from the store for ten days in 1957, it was the first time illness caused him to be away from his business in 68 years!

As a boy, Mr. Smith worked for James Wright, a gardener on East Broadway near Oakdale, for $3 a week. After that, he worked on the railroad for six years, first as a messenger boy and later as a clerk. In 1889, he took his $85 railroad salary, borrowed $500, and opened a store at 1004 Starr Avenue in partnership with his brother Fred. He proudly recalled, "We bought a horse and wagon for deliveries, and we paid the $500 back in six months." Two years later he bought out his brother's share of the partnership.

At that time, Starr Avenue was a plank road, and across the street where in a few years Von-Ewegen's drug store would be built, a cornfield stretched all the way to Kelsey Avenue and the ravine. Spring flooding often made it necessary to take a boat to the post office, then located on Front near Euclid, and Mr. Smith remembered seeing boats on Main Street as far up as Fourth.

In those early years, farmers brought in much of the merchandise sold in the store. Henry Comte, who farmed out on Pickle Road, brought butter and eggs. The eggs sold for 10 cents a dozen, or three dozen for a quarter.

The business prospered, and in 1892 Mr. Smith moved into a frame building at the familiar location of 918 Starr Avenue, where the store remained for over 85 years.

Because Mr. Smith could speak both German and French, he developed a large clientele among the newly-arrived farmers from those countries. He bought their produce and they bought his groceries. The business in those days was the typical pot-bellied stove, cracker-barrel store where customers came not only to shop, but also to swap gossip.

Mr. Smith recalled what the store was like at that time: "None of this self-serve stuff. We had to serve the customer. Climb up on big tall ladders to get tins off the top shelf. Grind coffee by hand. Scoop sugar out of a barrel onto the scales, then wrap it up in a paper parcel. No paper bags in those days, it was all brown paper and string."

In 1925 the business had again outgrown its building. At that time the large brick structure that most East Siders still remember was built on the same site, making Smith's the largest grocery in East Toledo. While the new store was being constructed, the business operated out of a building across the street at Starr and Platt.

The shopper could get some fine bargains during those early years at the Food Fair Market. Mr. Smith remembered that "coffee sold for 10 cents a pound, and the ladies all bought chicory to make the coffee stronger. Sugar was a nickel a pound, round steak 15 cents, potatoes 19 cents a bushel. And we had to give liver away." Smith's attracted loyal customers. There were several families he recalled who traded at the store for over 50 years.

E. J. Smith in his Food Fair Store.

Mr. Smith was an active member of the Knights of Columbus and the East Toledo Commercial Club, later the East Toledo Club. He lived in the house he built on the family homestead at 1208 Starr Avenue. The "Carlyle" apartment house, also on the property, was named for one of his sons. Eleven garages that housed his delivery trucks still stand behind the three houses on his original land.

Early Smith delivery truck.

Mr. Smith's wife Cora was a member of the well-known B. R. Baker family that lived nearby on Parker Street. She was said to have controlled the finances of the business, keeping it going during the Depression. When she died in 1955, they had been married for 62 years. Mr. Smith passed away in 1959 at the age of 92.

His three sons, Harold, Vernon, and Carlyle, had helped with the business over the years. After Mr. Smith's death, Harold continued to run the store along with his son, Richard, until it closed about 1980. The building was then torn down for the parking lot that now sits on the familiar location, but many East Siders still remember the legacy of hard work, fairness, and good service symbolized by businesses like E. J. Smith's Food Fair.

Chapter 6

DAYS OFF...

*

Parks and Amusements

from

Presque Isle

to

Pearson Park

*

PRESQUE ISLE: WHERE TOLEDO SPENT THE SUMMER

A century ago Northwest Ohio's most popular amusement park was Presque Isle, known as the Cedar Point of its day. People from all around the area would ride sixty miles or more on the train and six miles on a steamer from downtown Toledo just to spend four hours at what was called "the most beautiful and attractive resort and pleasure picnic grounds in the west."

Located on a small peninsula on the east shore of the river where the Port Authority now stands,

Presque Isle was accessible mainly by steamboat from downtown Toledo. The Pastime, Morning Star, and Evening Star all made frequent trips to the park loaded with passengers seeking to exchange the noise and heat of the city for the cool breezes off the Bay.

J. K. Tillotson, manager of the Presque Isle Park and Steamboat Company who also built the Hotel Victory at Put-in-Bay, developed the park in 1884. Before that it was used as a picnic area by those with private boats or by local residents out on the Navarre Tract of the Bay Shore. On August 8, 1876, Father Patrick O'Brien of Good Shepherd Parish brought 600 members of his church to Presque Isle. In 1881, the architect David Gibbs built "a very handsome and commodious bath and boat house" on the shore where the Bay curves to become the mouth of the Maumee River.

To make the park more attractive to his steamboat customers, Mr. Tillotson added a hotel, theater, dance pavilion, merry-go-round, Indian village, and restaurant. Soon there was also a busy midway, boardwalk, and Irish village to attract more visitors to Presque Isle, and Mr. Tillotson's steamboats were filled with passengers every day during the warm summer months.

The park also had one of the nation's first Ferris wheels, built just a couple years after George Ferris introduced the popular ride at the Columbian Exposition in Chicago in 1893. The Chicago wheel took over 2,100 riders to a height of 264 feet. The Ferris wheel at Presque Isle was much smaller, but still afforded its riders a breath-taking view of the whole park and surrounding waters of Maumee Bay.

Old photos show large crowds parading on Presque Isle's boardwalk or strolling down the midway to enjoy what one writer described as the "many pretentious buildings and dancing pavilions."

It was a place where young people came to meet. Helen Lang, a descendent of Peter Navarre, recalled how the young men would linger around the ticket booth whenever her future mother, the pretty Lena Mominee, worked there.   Other visitors came to Presque Isle just to enjoy the fresh air, fresh water, and famous fresh boiled eggs. Sometimes the crowds were so large that the steamboats would get stuck in the mud trying to leave the dock.

A dangerous episode took place at the steamship dock in June 1885. A large crowd had gathered to watch a mock naval battle being staged out in the Bay. The weight of so many people caused a piling to give way and the dock collapsed. Hundreds were hurtled into the water, including a mother with her two small babies. Fortunately, the water was not very deep and no one drowned in the accident.

Presque Isle.

It is recorded that on one day, July 4, 1888, there were 10,000 people at the park to celebrate the holiday. By that time the resort had become famous for its frog-leg suppers, vaudeville shows, and its "free opera." The dance floor band played such "spirited numbers" as "Mamma's Teeth Are Plugged With Zinc" and "Papa's Pants Will Soon Fit Willie." And on September 7, 1888, veterans of the Army of the Tennessee held their grand picnic at Presque Isle, and the main speaker was General William Tecumseh Sherman.

Presque Isle's heyday, however, was short-lived. In the end, the difficulty of reaching the park is what killed it. The popular Casino, which was built on the west side of the Maumee River in 1895, could be reached by a short streetcar ride out Summit Street. As the crowds at Presque Isle diminished, Mr. Tillotson's steamboat company went bankrupt, and shortly after the turn of the century the once-thriving "Cedar Point of its day" was abandoned.

In the late 1920s and early 1930s the industrial potential of the land out on the Bay Shore was realized. The C & O railroad lines and the Hocking Valley coal and iron ore docks were built. Today the huge Port Authority docks have completely removed all traces of the former amusement park and even altered the shape of the whole Presque Isle peninsula from which the park had received its French name.

Fortunately, a photographer who lived on the Bay Shore, Cleo Keller, has preserved the memory of Presque Isle in several pictures taken during the 1890s. When looking at these early photographs, it is almost possible to hear again the steamboats puffing up to the dock and to feel the fresh breezes blowing off the Bay at what was once the most popular amusement park in Northwest Ohio.

PRENTICE PARK: THE OLDEST PARK IN TOLEDO

The surprising discovery was made recently that humble little Prentice Park on the East Side is the oldest park in Toledo. Most histories name City Park (now Savage Park), which was donated by the Lenk brewing family in 1871, as the city's first park. But early transfer cards confirm that Prentice Park is thirteen years older.

The triangular, neighborhood park is named for the first white child born in what became downtown Toledo, Frederick Prentice, who was one of the donors of the land. One of the streets that runs beside the park is also named after Mr. Prentice.

In the 1850s, three new plats were laid out on the East Side. One of those, the Williams' plat, extended from Navarre Avenue to Nevada Street and from Oak to near Federal Street. City real estate records show that on April 26, 1858, William S. Williams, Charles Conahan, and Frederick Prentice granted part of their land to be used as a "Village Green," as it is clearly labelled on the plat map. No other land in Toledo since that time has remained in continuous use as a park.

Today the park has a grass-infield baseball diamond, two sets of swings, two basketball hoops, and a wooden gazebo built about 1970. It is in need of some benches, some trash barrels, and some general upgrading. The gazebo needs paint, and graffiti needs to be removed from several areas, including the park sign.

Even though this little "flat-iron" park is practically unknown to the rest of the city, including many people living on the East Side, it should not be neglected. Perhaps the discovery that it is indeed the oldest park in Toledo will stimulate interest in maintaining it as a natural attraction of the neighborhood, which is what the city's first parks were meant to be.

PETER NAVARRE SHARES HISTORY OF NAVARRE PARK

The celebration of Peter Navarre Day on September 9, 1989, recalls the close connection between the famous pioneer scout and the East Side park that bears his name.

Navarre Park was developed during the 1890s on land formerly owned by Oliver Stevens, which also included most of what is now Sun Oil property. The naturally hilly region was thought to be an ideal setting for a park. An early description of the park's "rustic beauty and natural simplicity" calls it "one of the most beautiful parks, not only in the city of Toledo, but in the whole State of Ohio."

An early shelter house was built on the high ground in 1895. There was also a pavilion where band concerts were held on summer Sunday afternoons and evenings. The first shelter house was replaced by the current structure during the W.P.A. building programs of the 1930s.

Early accounts of the park also speak of a statue of Peter Navarre in pioneer clothing near one of the entrances. No picture or trace of this statue, however, has come to light. The Navarre Monument, still standing on the corner of Navarre and White Street, was dedicated at a special 4th of July celebration in 1914.

On September 9th, 1922, a Peter Navarre Day was declared and the restored 1860s Navarre family cabin was brought to the park from the Enos Mominee farm out Seaman Road. It was on September 9th, 1813, that Navarre delivered the famous message from General Harrison at Fort Meigs to Commodore Perry to engage the British fleet, resulting in the Battle of Lake Erie the next day. The cabin is now standing at Toledo Botanical Gardens as an example of a pioneer homestead.

Pavilion, Navarre Park, Toledo, Ohio.

First Shelter House, built 1895.

Over the years, Navarre Park has continued to serve East Side residents. In the early days, regular instructors taught recreation classes at the park. Miss Ruth Farrell instructed the girls in various activities, and Mr. James Wickenden taught baseball, basketball, and croquet to boys. Later, a swimming pool, baseball and softball diamonds, and tennis courts were added.

The park has changed in many ways. A newspaper account in 1922 spoke of its green hills that "wave over throngs of happy picnickers, echoing the laughter of little children, and bending caressingly over the weary, filling them with renewed vigor." In recent years those "green arenas" have suffered from vandalism and neglect and shortages of tax dollars, so that the weary had to fend for themselves.

But once again the park is showing signs of new life. The shelter house has been modernized and is now used as a thriving Senior Center. The resurfaced tennis courts, the ball diamonds, swimming pool, and play areas are all used extensively. And the Family Center, also located at the park, provides many services to the East Side community.

In 1989, Peter Navarre Day was again celebrated, and a new plaque for the monument was dedicated by the East Toledo Historical Society. A renewed interest in Peter Navarre and his important role in the history of this area has gone hand-in-hand with the renewed vitality of Navarre Park.

THE BEGINNING OF PEARSON PARK

It all started with a casual conversation on Main Street. Now, nearly 60 years after its dedication, Pearson Park is still one of the most popular Metroparks in the Toledo area.

One day, in the law offices of D. H. James, George Pearson was writing a story. Mr. Pearson, a Blade reporter who wrote the East Side column for 52 years, had been discussing with his friend a tract of 320 acres out Navarre Avenue known as the bank lands. The land had been owned by the railroads, but various banks now held mortgage claims on it.

Both men believed that this last big tract of forest between Toledo and Port Clinton should be saved for a nature park rather than cut down for timber. So Mr. Pearson wrote a story, then another. Finally his series of articles began to arouse public interest in saving the endangered forest land.

Meanwhile, the reporter was tipped off by Anton Munding, a nature lover from Oregon Township, that trees were being cut down. Owners of the land were not only clearing away dead timber, but also had chopped down 1,200 live trees. Mr. Pearson wrote another series of stories, urging someone to come to the rescue.

The Toledo Metropolitan Park Board read the articles and became interested, along with other civic-minded citizens. Claims on a defunct bank

which held the mortgage on 280 acres were initiated.
The park board then made a bid for the property
and was able to obtain it. Then the East Toledo Club
successfully organized a plan to get the remaining
40 acres. Finally, in 1934, "to the surprise of no one
but himself," the park was named for Mr. Pearson.

The New Deal programs of the 1930s provided
workers to develop the park. A series of ponds
were dug and lined with stone, a shelter house built,
trails laid out, and several smaller structures
constructed. The park continued to grow, and even
included horse trails and an outdoor roller-skating
rink at one time.

Today, the ball diamonds, walking trails,
tennis courts, playgrounds, and nature areas are
being used more than ever by people of all ages.
And the Packer-Hammersmith Center at the
remodeled shelter house now provides a way to
observe wildlife in a natural setting. Across from
the nature center stands a large boulder found in
the park. A plaque on the boulder is dedicated to
George Pearson, a man who initiated dozens of East
Side projects but none more important than his
effort to save Pearson Park.

Chapter 7

GEMS OF THE COMMUNITY...

*

Churches and Schools

from

Pioneer Times

to

The Present

*

EAST TOLEDO'S FIRST CHURCHES

On October 28, 1849, the First Congregational Church of Oregon Township met at the home of Horace Howland on what is now Consaul Street. At that time all of East Toledo was called "Utah," and was part of Oregon Township. The charter members of the church were of the Denman, Brown, and Howland families who lived in that area.

In 1850 a small log church was built at the corner of Consaul Street and Otter Creek Road. A marker on the site was planned for Toledo's centennial in 1937, but no such commemorative was ever placed there. Rev. Ezra Howland was chosen as pastor and services were held in the little church until the outbreak of the Civil War.

When the call for troops went out, every male member of the church enlisted except the aged pastor. After the war, in September 1868, the church reorganized as Second Congregational, and constructed a frame building on Fourth Street near Euclid. Most of the East Side was still woods and fields, and the central business area was at Front and Euclid (then called Cherry Street).

The first pastor of this church was Rev. Robert Quaife. He was the father of John Quaife, former superintendent of Postal Station A. The congregation grew, and the large brick church that still remains on the site was built in the early 1890s. A bulletin from 1909 lists as members such prominent East Siders as Herman Gross, W.F. Barrett, D. Harry Harpster, T.J. Torrence, William Davies, Charles Weiler, Claud Gettings, and George Pearson.

* * *

The first church organized within the present boundaries of East Toledo was the Second Baptist Church on January 10, 1864. The first building, dedicated two years later, was located at the corner of Fourth and Steadman where the stone row-houses now stand. The Cranes and Whitmores were among the early members, as were Elias Fassett and Elijah Woodruff. The current stone church at Main and Greenwood was built in 1907.

Also during the Civil War, a brick "Union" church was built in the Fassett Street area. In 1872 it was sold to the Pennsylvania Railroad and was later used as a roundhouse. The following year Memorial Baptist was built at Oak and Hathaway where it still stands, bearing the engraved inscription "Dawson Chapel, 1873." Rev. Samuel Dawson, for whom Dawson Street was named, was pastor of Union Church, Memorial Baptist, and also Second Baptist until his death in 1875.

* * *

Among other early East Side churches, St. Louis Parish was organized by French Catholic families who built their church at its present location on Sixth Street. Many prominent East Toledoans went there, including the Gladieuxs, Navarres, Metzgers, Montvilles, and Plumeys. Good Shepherd was started in 1872 and the first church was built on Clark Street in 1873. The current church dates to Father O'Brien's time at the turn of the century.

In 1883, part of the Cherry Street Bridge was washed away. This led the German Catholics who attended St. Mary's downtown to organize Sacred Heart Parish and the German Lutherans who attended St. Paul's to organize St. Mark's. The first Sacred Heart Church was built in 1883 and burned in 1900, the year the present church was built. St. Mark Lutheran dates to 1884, and the current building to 1916.

Salem German M.E. Church, located at Nevada and Federal, celebrated their 100th anniversary in 1989, and Clark Street Methodist held their centennial on April 27th of the following year. Rev. Harold Black was pastor of both churches during the time of their centennial celebrations. Martin Luther, at Nevada and Arden Place, also marked their 100th anniversary that year, their congregation being organized on September 20, 1890.

Other churches dating from the 1800's include the Birmingham Congregational Church, organized April 21, 1893, and the East Side Presbyterian

First St. John's, Seaman Rd. in 1928.

St. Paul Episcopal, 4th & Euclid. Burned 3/13/51.

Society that began meeting on February 18, 1894, at
Foresters Hall in the Weber Block. The
Presbyterians built a church at Starr and Garfield
Place about 1907. This church burned in 1930, at
which time they merged with Eastminster
Presbyterian on the corner of Navarre and
Woodville. The East Side Professional Building was
built on the foundations of the old church.

Another spectacular fire destroyed St. Paul's
Episcopal Church in 1951. The cornerstone of that
church, which stood on the northwest corner of
Fourth and Euclid, was laid on May 16, 1889. After
the fire, the congregation rebuilt out on Coy Road.

All these churches and many others that
began in the 20th century have flourished on the
East Side and served the community well. Our city
has been called Holy Toledo because of its many
churches, and the East Side has had more than its
share of fine congregations. Perhaps a marker
should be placed on the site of that first log church
at Consaul and Otter Creek Road where it all started
nearly 150 years ago.

TWO METHODIST CHURCHES CELEBRATE CENTENNIALS

The growing pains and the accomplishments of
churches started on the East Side during the last
years of the 19th century can be seen in the history
of two congregations that were organized within a
year of each other. Salem United Methodist was
dedicated on May 19, 1889, and Clark Street
Methodist dates from April 27, 1890.

Salem United Methodist constructed a 28 x 40
foot sanctuary in 1889 on their lot at the corner of
Federal and Nevada Streets, which they had

purchased for $400. Early records show the cost of
materials and labor a century ago: $49.40 for
bricks, $10.45 for sheet metal for the tower, $216.13
for carpentry, $109.85 for plaster and plastering,
$70 for an organ, $17 for a bookcase, and $2 for an
extra table.   Five years later, the pastor's annual
salary was given as $550.

A number of distinguished ministers served
the congregation over the years.   Rev. John
Holtcamp, a native of Elmore, Ohio, and graduate of
Baldwin-Wallace College, was pastor from 1907 to
1915. Under his leadership the current building was
constructed in 1908 at a cost of about $3,000. Pastor
Holtcamp was in the ministry for a total of 46 years,
and is said to have preached 4,679 sermons.

The church continued to grow under Rev.
Bockstahler and his successors.   On May 28, 1925,
the church board voted to hold services in both
German and English, and after 1928 all services were
changed to English.   Names like Nietz, Flegle,
Ashbaucher, Siewert, DeShetler, and Cummins were
some of the active families during the 1920s and 30s.

Rev. Harry Troutner and Rev. Albert Mathias
served the church from 1951 to 1968, and the
congregation reached its highest membership totals
during this time. The sanctuary was remodeled, and
work was also done on the church building and the
parsonage at 840 Main Street.   Rev. Black became
pastor in 1985.

Rev. Black's other congregation at 1133 Clark
Street began as a Sunday School organized by
members of an early Methodist Church located at
Euclid and Third Street.   In 1890, a 30 x 50 foot
building was constructed on Clark Street at a cost
of $3,245.37. Rev. C. B. Holding was the first pastor,
and there were 56 names on the rolls, mostly by
letter of transfer from other churches.   The first
letter was from James L. Stark who transferred from

Broadway Methodist.

The congregation grew rapidly and a new church, the current building, was finished in 1903. A. E. Forster was the building chairman, Joseph Pheils was the contractor, and Langdon and Hohly the architects. Rev. Mortimore Gascoigne was pastor when the new church was built.

On Sunday morning, February 2, 1919, sparks from the chimney set fire to the roof of the church and the whole upper part was destroyed. Fortunately, no one attending the Sunday School classes at the time was injured. When the repairs were all finished, $8,000 more than the insurance settlement had been spent.

Clark St. Methodist.

Many ministers have served the congregation, with Rev. William Nungester holding the longest tenure of 14 years. When the area began to experience economic decline, the church reached out to the neighborhood and promoted Head Start programs in 1965. The church also became a meeting place for the Neighborhood Improvement group.

During their recent centennial celebrations both churches have displayed early memorabilia and printed historical booklets, as have many other East Side congregations, recalling their service to the people of the community over the years.

HEATHERDOWNS CHURCH HAS EAST SIDE ROOTS

A whole book could be written on the history of all the churches east of the river, and many of those congregational histories are available elsewhere. But it is generally not known that a large church on Byrne Road near Glendale, Heatherdowns Church of the Brethren, had its beginnings on the East Side.

In 1907, Warren and Alsada Kaser started holding Sunday School and prayer meetings in their home at 628 Leonard Street. "Sadie," the mother of eight children, also provided Sunday dinner for all who attended and for the visiting minister who otherwise received no money for his services.

Alsada Kaser was born on a farm near Sherwood, Ohio, in 1870, and was known by all as a very devout woman. It was said that when she went shopping with her children, she wouldn't let them pick up a straight pin off the floor. She told them it would be like stealing, because the pin didn't belong to them.

She was always willing to share anything she had. One of her relatives used to keep the good silverware, doilies, and dishes put away and never used them. When the house burned down, all those unused things were lost. Sadie decided that would never happen to her, and all her possessions, no matter how valuable, would be put to use.

By April of 1909, the District Mission Board arranged for space for the fledgling church in a building at the corner of Oak and Greenwood, where informal meetings continued for the next four years. In good weather, services were often held at Navarre Park.

In 1913 seventeen people pledged monthly contributions to rent an "upper room" at the ice house at Nevada and Parker Streets, where the First Toledo Church of the Brethren was officially organized on August 1, 1914. It was said that Rev. Nathan McKimmy, the Pastor and Elder at the time, could "fire up a good sermon" to take the chill off using the old ice house for worship.

When the small congregation celebrated their first Communion service on May 23, 1914, Alsada Kaser was not there. She was too sick to attend. She died of cancer three months later on August 14th, at the age of 44.

But the church she had helped to start would continue to grow. By 1921 a new building was completed on Woodville Road between Varland and East Broadway. Inside the cornerstone was placed the well-worn Bible of Alsada Kaser.

Thirty-five years later the congregation had outgrown its building and three acres of land was purchased out Byrne Road. The renamed Heatherdowns Church of the Brethren worshipped in a new $115,000 building for the first time on January 26, 1959. Alsada Kaser of Leonard Street had built well.

EARLY DAYS OF FRANKLIN SCHOOL

In addition to its many fine churches, which are truly gems of the community, the East Side also has many outstanding school buildings, topped off by the imposing Waite High School campus. Most of the elementary schools have a history similar to that of Franklin, the first large grade school on the East Side.

The very first school on the East Side was on the river bank near where Tony Packo's now stands on Consaul Street. Mrs. Mary Berry was the teacher of the 15 pupils who first met in that log building in May 1837. She taught from 9 to 4 Monday through Friday and on alternate Saturdays. For this she was paid a salary of $1.50 a week. By 1839, Mrs. Berry was also teaching in a "board shanty" on Front Street near Cherry (Euclid).

"In the early 1850s the children of Utah, as East Toledo was then called, gathered in a little building at the corner of Oak and First streets," writes Louise Bitter, who along with Maria Farst recorded the history of the East Side's first schools. One teacher at that early school was Alonzo Rogers, and another was Ambrose Eggleston who also taught in a log school house in the vicinity of Oak and Fassett Street.

A few years later, in 1855, the newly formed Board of Education purchased two lots where the present Franklin School is now located. A two-story frame structure was built that year, and a second wooden building was erected in 1866. Also, on the same site, a small brick building formerly occupied by the late James Raymer, was purchased for the teaching of German.

The little wooden school that housed the primary students had rows of long green benches with inverted boxes to hold the students' books. There was seating capacity for 80 children, and the school was crowded to the limit. Heat was provided by a cord-wood stove at one end of each room.

Soon it was apparent a larger school was needed, and a $2000 six-room, three-story brick building opened in January of 1872. The frame buildings were sold, but the little brick structure continued to be used for German classes. From the new school's third floor windows students could watch the flash and hear the boom of the 100 cannon salute celebrating the appointment of Morrison R. Waite as Chief Justice of the Supreme Court in 1874.

Six rooms were added to the east end of the school about 1881, and the little brick German classroom became the janitor's residence. This was the time of East Toledo's population boom, and during the 1880s and 1890s the first Raymer, Navarre, East Side Central, and Birmingham schools were built. In 1897 another six-room addition was made to Franklin School.

George Long, who attended Franklin from 1865 to 1874, recalled some of the exploits of his former classmates. Parks Hone, later a Toledo police judge, appeared at school one day with leather sewed on the seat of his pants. His mother was tired of constantly sewing patches that were worn off sliding down a nearby hill on barrel staves.

Another classmate was "Danger" O'Brien. He got his nickname by accepting a dare to climb up the spar of a sailing vessel docked along the river.

He accomplished the feat and then stood on his head at the top of the mast.

Old Franklin School, 1923.

It was at Franklin School that Miss Virginia Nauts pioneered the first Kindergarten program. Another teacher, Miss Abbie Card, became the wife of Rev. Osborne, a pastor at Second Baptist Church which then stood across Steadman Street where the stone row-houses are now located. Many of those first teachers bought lots together when South Sixth Street (now Arden Place) was being developed.

One of the first principals at Franklin was Miss McNeil. She later became a missionary when she married the United States Consul to China. Other early principals were Miss Lawton, Miss Mattie Mettler, Homer Stone, Mr. Turner, Mr. R. C. VanGorder, and Miss Belle Schuh.

The VanGorder name holds a special distinction at Franklin School. R. C. VanGorder became principal in 1888, and served in that capacity for 40 years. Then, a few years later, his son Henry VanGorder also became principal of Franklin, and remained there until the 1960s. Together, father and son were principals for 64 years.

By the 1920s the East Side was still growing rapidly, and several of the early grade schools were severely overcrowded. The old Franklin School was replaced in 1924 by the modern brick building that still stands at the same location. The current Navarre, Raymer, and Birmingham schools, as well as the new Garfield and Oakdale schools, were all built within a decade.

Old East Side Central was replaced by a new building in 1960, and the East Side Junior High is an even more recent building. Sacred Heart School, built in 1889 and remodelled in 1954, is still in use today, one of many East Side parochial schools.

?ACHER STARTED BUSINESS CLASSES IN TOLEDO SCHOOLS

Melvin B. Severance, whose long life began before Lincoln was elected president and lasted almost until the start of the Second World War, is credited with teaching the first typing and shorthand classes in the Toledo public schools. Later in his career, he was known as the Father of Waite High School.

Mr. Severance was born in Norfolk, Ontario, and received his first teaching certificate at the age of 18. After teaching in a country school for seven years, he came to Ypsilanti, Michigan, and completed a four-year college course in two years at the old Michigan State Normal College. He arrived in Toledo in 1888, and began teaching at the Cleary Business College.

In 1895, Mr. Severance opened his own school, the East Side Business College, which was located on the second floor of the Weber Block at Front and Main. Some traces of this school, such as the old "Office" sign on the wall, could still be seen in the long-deserted hallways of the building when it was recently being restored as a modern business incubator for University of Toledo students.

After operating the business college for three years, Mr. Severance was induced by Superintendent W. W. Chalmers to initiate the first commercial courses in the old Toledo High School at Michigan and Adams. He therefore sold the East Side Business College to Mr. M. H. Davis, and through many transformations it is still in operation today as the Davis Business College.

His first shorthand and typing classes in the public schools were so large that Mr. Severance would have to dictate to one group while another group was typing. Teaching under these conditions was very demanding and was also very taxing on his voice. So when he was offered the job of chief city accountant by Mayor Brand Whitlock, he accepted.

In 1912, he returned to teaching his courses at the old Central High School. But when Waite was opened in 1914, Mr. Severance went with several other teachers to the new school to organize the commercial department there. He remained at Waite for the next 17 years, retiring in June of 1931, at the age of 70, as required by law. During that time he also worked for the Toledo Chapter of the American Institute of Banking as instructor in advanced banking, economics, investments, and credits.

His wife, Nellie, passed away in 1935, and Mr. Severance's health began to decline as he approached the age of 80. In his last years he lived at the house of his son, Melvin, Jr., at 627 East Broadway, where he died on June 4, 1940. During his whole working life, he missed only six days because of illness.

As a final tribute to him, it has been noted that throughout his long career, Mr. Severance "never was out of employment, never sought a position, and never received a word of criticism from any one who was supervising his work."

Many other outstanding teachers, like Mr. Severance, have served Waite High School over the years. Most East Siders can recall certain favorite instructors, many of whom taught more than one generation of Waite students.

Also, Waite has had a progression of dedicated principals: Charles Gayman, James Pollock, Philip Conser, Christian Thomson, Leonard Hendrickson, Richard McNeill, Lew Cross, Steve Contos, and Ric Cervantes. Over 75 years after its first entering class, Waite High School remains one of the true gems of the East Side.

LIFE AT WAITE HIGH SCHOOL IN THE 1920s

Early issues of the <u>Retina</u>, a student "magazine portraying the life and events" at Waite High School, give an interesting view of what life

was like for those who attended the school during
the 1920s. The following items are a few glimpses
seen through several Retinas published between
1923 and 1926.

Knute Rockne, the famous football coach at
Notre Dame, gave a talk in Toledo in 1925. The
March issue of the Retina reports that he spoke
against "the fellow who goes to college merely for
the dances he can attend and the dates he can get,"
and that "lounge lizards" do nothing to help
themselves or their schools. Rockne concluded that
"the good citizens of the future" will not come from
such fellows. No mention was made, however, of the
Gipper.

The same March 1925 issue also discussed the
building of the stadium. Even though the Waite Bowl
was called "one of the best football fields in the
country," the Board of Education "displayed a fine,
forward-looking spirit" by filling in the ravine
between East Broadway and White Street (now Elgin)
for use as a "gridiron, track, and baseball field."
Finished several years later, the Waite Stadium
remains the best high school football field in the
city.

Several Retinas had news of Waite alumni. The
October 1924 issue recorded that Ted Lamb had
graduated from Dartmouth College and entered the
Harvard Law School. Cornelia Harpster (now
Palmer), who had been attending the University of
Toledo, enrolled at Ohio University at Athens.
Myron Textor was studying Osteopathy at Kirksville,
Missouri. Anna Lou Wells was in the top 10% of her
class at Oberlin, and Pauline Odom and Bill Greiner
were "taking post graduate work at Waite." Alice
Nauts had made the freshman hockey team at
Wisconsin.

How faculty members spent their summers was
of interest to Retina reporters. In 1924, Mr. Lutz

conducted geological excursions to Kelley's Island,
Miss Wemp went to the Catskills, and Mr. Jaeger
"studied the relationship of paint to metal." It was
reported that Miss Roache and Miss Griffith taught
"ignerant peepul" from the four high schools, and
that Mr. Ehrle "collected a coat of tan, fifteen
pounds of avoirdupois, and some basketball 'dope' at
Ann Arbor."

The Retina was also a literary magazine for
the school. Monthly activities were recorded for the
women's Zetas and Pericleans and the men's Forum
and Quill & Dagger Literary Societies. One issue
recalled the history of the Forum, which started in
1906 at the old East Side High School (a part of East
Side Central). The Forum Literary Society was
founded by Mr. Rex Wells to promote public speaking
and debating skills. John Baymiller, the 1924 Forum
"censor of the year," had mapped out a program
emphasizing debate, biography, and drama. The
literary editors for the Retina during these years
were Betty Kendall, Dorothy Briggs, and Mark
Winchester.

Waite had good football teams in the mid-
1920s, with Pete Pencoff at quarterback and Ben
Pencheff at halfback during these issues of the
Retina. The 1924 team won the championship,
defeating Scott 13-6 on Thanksgiving Day in the
Bowl. Then on December 6th, the "purple hurricane"
beat a team from Boston by the score of 46-0. That
team finished 10-0, outscoring their opponents by a
total of 419-61, including a 90-0 victory over
Morenci.

Also in 1924, former Waite football players
Dutch Stamman, Dwight Keller, and Vic Domhoff had
made the varsity team at the University of Michigan.
In 1926, the basketball team at Waite won the city
championship with a 25-20 victory over Woodward in
the last game.

Another feature of the Retina was a comic page, sometimes called "Morrison R. Wit." A sample of a 1920s thigh-slapper went: "Every time I hear that tune it haunts me." Reply: "Why shouldn't it? You murdered it." Another joke goes: "Has your brother come home from college for the holidays yet?" Answer: "I guess so; or else my car has been stolen."

Occasionally a short poem appeared on the comic page:

> I mix my beans with honey,
> I've done so all my life.
> They taste a little funny,
> But it keeps them on my knife.

Thumbing through these magazines gives a more detailed view of high school life than appeared either in the yearbook or the trophy case. The fabric of day-to-day life almost 70 years ago comes alive again when "seen" through the pages of the Waite Retina.

A BRIEF HISTORY OF ATHLETICS AT WAITE

Waite High School has a truly remarkable tradition of athletic excellence. Between 1921 and 1963 the football team won or tied for eighteen City Championships, winning the City League over 40% of the time! During the decade of the 1930s, Waite was City Champs an unbelievable eight out of ten years. The undefeated 1932 team outscored its opponents 401-16, and the 1939 team also won the State Championship.

But football is not the only sport in which

Waite teams have excelled. The basketball team won
the Northwest Ohio Championship as early as 1915.
It won the City Championship again in 1924 and 1932.
As recently as 1973–74 it won the Blue Division
Championship when Gary Jackson scored 366 points
that season. There have also been many fine girls'
basketball teams as well, and in 1987–88 Tammy
Lorton won the city scoring championship.

Waite baseball teams have been City Champs
many times. In 1945, Steve Contos led the team in
home runs. During the 1982 season, pitcher Dan
Boening was City League Player of the Year. The
hockey team won five consecutive divisional titles
during the late 1970s, finishing third in the state in
1976–77.

There also have been several outstanding
tennis teams and track teams at Waite. In addition,
the cross-country team achieved a phenomenal
record in the 1940s and early 1950s. Those teams
won ten out of twelve City Championships and seven
out of twelve District Championships. Neil Burson
won three straight Ohio Scholastic Conference meets,
and during his senior year shaved thirty seconds
off the state record.

So many other names of individual Waite stars
come back from the past: Ted Keller, Boni Petcoff,
Carl Stamman, Dodge Alexander, Francis Lengel, Red
Snider, Claire Dunn, Bob and Harold Hecklinger,
Danny Marazon, Bill Gregus, Pete Stoner, Stan
Starkey, Rick Fields, Jack Romp, Curtis Johnson,
Dick Chisholm, Bob Parks, Louis Breuer, Jesse
Pettaway, Mark Kerr, and many more too numerous
to list. Each person remembers his or her own
heroes. There have been many excellent coaches
too, including Larry Bevan, Don McCallister, Jack
Mollenkopf (later at Purdue), Frank Pauly, Pete
Fanning, and (the author's favorite) Jack O'Connell.

Waite also has outstanding athletic facilities.

Waite Stadium, dedicated in 1934, is still one of the finest high school athletic fields. It was designed by Forster, Wernert, and Taylor, local engineers, and was built for about $100,000 with the Civil Works Administration providing over half of the cost. It is now named in honor of Coach Jack Mollenkopf. The 24,000 square-foot Field House was dedicated on May 3, 1954, and cost $709,000. It is named in honor of long-time school board member from the East Side, Grant Murray.

The Waite Bowl, circa 1920.

In the early years, Waite had a national reputation, especially in football. The 1923 team traveled to Buffalo, Terre Haute, Columbus, Cleveland, and Louisville. That year they beat Woodward 68-0 and Columbus West 115-0. As late as 1940, the team went to Portland, Oregon, for a game. The toughest competition was often right in Toledo

when Waite played Scott in the traditional
Thanksgiving Day game. Win or lose, Waite High
School can be proud of its outstanding athletic
heritage, and also of its many fine student-athletes.

SOME HIGHLIGHTS OF WAITE'S ATHLETIC HISTORY

<u>1914, Thanksgiving Day</u>: First Waite-Scott football
game. Waite wins.

<u>Sept. 29, 1917</u>: First football game played in Waite
Bowl. Waite 38, Monroe 0.

<u>March 1920</u>: Tennis team organized as four new
courts are built.

<u>1921</u>: Football team wins first City Championship with
a 10-1 record, outscoring opponents 666-31.

<u>Oct. 28, 1922</u>: Heavyweight champ Jack Dempsey
attends Waite football game.

<u>1924</u>: Baseball team goes 12-0 with seven players on
All-Star Team.

<u>March 19, 1931</u>: New football coach Don McCallister
begins his first spring practice.

<u>1931-32</u>: Basketball team wins City Championship
with a 15-1 record.

<u>1932</u>: The name "Golden Tornadoes" is officially
changed to "Waite Indians."

<u>Sept. 21, 1934</u>: Waite Stadium is dedicated.

<u>1935:</u>　Red Snider, All-City football player, leads city in scoring.　Jack Mollenkopf becomes coach.

<u>April 12, 1939:</u>　Baseball game postponed by snow.

<u>1945:</u>　Lew Cross leads baseball team in pitching; Steve Contos leads in home runs.

<u>1947:</u>　Football team wins City Championship.　Waite Band plays at Browns and Lions games.

<u>1948-49:</u>　Track team sets five school records.

<u>1952-53:</u>　Cross-country team wins fifth straight City and District Titles.　Neil Burson finishes first for third year in a row, breaking the state record by thirty seconds.

<u>May 3, 1954:</u>　Grant Murray Fieldhouse is dedicated.

<u>1963:</u>　Football team wins 18th and last City Title. Night football is banned.

<u>1969:</u>　Basketball team wins its 500th game.

<u>1979-80:</u>　Hockey team wins fifth consecutive division title.

<u>1985-86:</u>　Mark Kerr is first State Wrestling Champ.

<u>1987-88:</u>　Tammy Lorton wins City League scoring title　in Girls' Basketball.

<u>1989-90:</u>　Joe Guerrero, Charles Delker, Kevin Horn, and Richard Kuzma win Coach of Year honors.

Chapter 8

EAST SIDERS...

*

Other Interesting People

from

Civic Leaders

to

Ordinary Citizens

*

PROMINENT EAST SIDERS OF 50 YEARS AGO

The recent death in Hollywood of John Ehrle, the Waite graduate who became a well-known performer, calls attention to a George Pearson article of 1941 with the headline: "John Ehrle's Rise Suggests Other East Siders' Success."

Beginning with Mr. Ehrle's success in starting the Toledo Civic Opera and his other performing achievements, the article then calls the roll of a surprising number of East Siders who held important positions in the city just prior to the bombing of Pearl Harbor over fifty years ago.

In government, Frank I. Consaul, who lived at the corner of Euclid and Greenwood, and Arthur Jurrus were City Councilmen. Samuel Campbell was a member of the Toledo Port Commission, just as East Sider Gary Failor later headed the Toledo Port Authority. George Lumm was on the Civil Service Commission in 1941, and Max Shepherst was secretary, treasurer and landscape architect of the Metropolitan Park Board.

In addition, Gordon Jeffrey, who was a graduate of Waite and Ohio State University, was welfare director, Paul Robinette was traffic commissioner, Edward Hoffman was traffic inspector, and Bernard Kesting, whose family built the beautiful stone house at East Broadway and Mott, was Lucas County engineer.

A former Ironville boy, Carl Belkofer, was president of the Junior Chamber of Commerce, and Art Gratop was an important member of the Chamber. William Wright, one of John Gunckel's original "Old Newsboys" who had to support himself from the age of 12, was president of the Toledo Community Chest. Ray Loftus, the Community Chest's superintendent, was also secretary of the Toledo Rotary Club, and Hoyt Boden, another East Toledoan, was on the Public Library Board.

The list goes on. Charles Webb and Amos Conn (an interestingly named attorney) both served as governors of the Exchange Club. Frank Wiley was president of the Toledo Methodist Men's organization, a position also formerly held by Fred Klag of Waite High School. Another well-known East Side attorney, Mark Winchester, who lived at Euclid and Coney Court, was president of the Toledo Sunday School Association. And Rev. Harlan Frost of Second Baptist Church was the executive secretary of the Toledo Council of Churches.

In professional circles of fifty years ago, Dr. M. R. Lorenzen practiced at Euclid and 6th Street, and Drs. Boni Petcoff, Rollin Kuebbeler, Horace Beckwith, and Paul Black were all East Side men. Dr. Clarence Ordway spent his life as a doctor and surgeon on the East Side and developed East Toledo's first hospital on Oak Street in the early 1900s.

Ralph Millard, of the Millard Avenue family, a president of the East Toledo Club, was also president of the Toledo Automobile Club and member of the Board of Education. Charles Kirk, superintendent of Station A, later became Postmaster of Toledo. And Fern Kettel, another East Sider, was Vice-President of the Lamson Brothers Company in 1941.

Finally, among Toledo educators, Merritt Nauts, principal of DeVilbiss fifty years ago, was from the East Side. And Ralph Dugdale, former principal at Navarre, went on to become superintendent of schools both in Toledo and in Portland, Oregon. Jack Mollenkopf, football coach at Waite, would also go on to be head coach at Purdue University.

The roll call could continue. But this partial list shows the extent that East Siders were involved in important positions at just this one particular point in time. It is gratifying to share George Pearson's pride that over the years many others born east of the river have made significant contributions to the society in which they lived, and that they continue to do so today.

THE BROWNS OF MIAMI STREET

A hundred years ago the twin mansions of
Daniel and Stillman Brown stood overlooking the
Maumee River on Miami Street in East Toledo. Built
in 1870 by the two family members who owned the
prosperous stockyards, the mansions were mentioned
as East Side landmarks in many early histories of
Toledo.

Brown Mansions, built 1870. From 1875 Directory.

Daniel and Stillman Brown came to East Toledo in 1859 from Montgomery, Vermont, and bought the stockyards that stood where the Weiler Homes is today. The business grew rapidly. All animals shipped from Chicago were unloaded and fed in Toledo. As many as 300 railroad cars a day brought animals to the stockyards, and each year between 15,000 and 25,000 hogs were butchered there.

The Browns soon added to their enterprises. In the next couple of years Daniel opened the first general store in the area, and Stillman built a large hotel on the other side of the railroad tracks. It is not recorded if the guests ever complained about the accompanying aroma, but the hotel seems to have done well.

Their prosperity enabled the Browns to build the impressive Italianate homes side by side above the riverbank on Miami Street. The three-story brick mansions had identical towers and mansard roofs, and also the heavy eye-brow window hoods typical of late 19th-century Italianate architecture.

The Browns joined other pioneer East Side families like the Fassetts, Chamberlins, Whitmores, Cranes, and Chesbroughs in taking advantage of the natural beauty of the river setting. Later, when smoke from the railroads and steamboats made these homes less desirable, prosperous East Siders built their mansions further up the river between Rossford and Perrysburg.

Daniel Brown died of cancer in 1896 and Stillman passed away just four years later. Stillman's home at 639 Miami disappeared from the City Directories in 1924 and was probably torn down at that time. Daniel Brown's widow remained in the other home for many years, and the old mansion survived until 1946 when it burned to the ground. Today the Jobst Institute occupies the site where the two mansions once stood.

CAPT. JOHN CRAIG: TOLEDO'S EARLY SHIPBUILDER

John Craig was born on Christmas day just one year after two tiny communities along the Maumee River merged to become the city of Toledo. By the time of his death 95 years later in 1934, he had witnessed many changes in the city he adopted, and his Craig Shipbuilding Company on the East Side had constructed 107 Great Lakes vessels.

Born in New York City in 1838, Craig was the son of a ship's sawyer. He attended college in New York and entered the ship construction business there. During the Civil War he remodeled 23 merchant craft into gunboats and mortar boats. The Winona, one of the gunboats, was delivered only 63 days after the contract was signed.

After building boats in the Great Lakes area for several years, he came to Toledo and organized Craig Shipbuilding on Front Street in 1889. It was the busiest shipyard of the time, turning out several lake vessels every year. Nearing the age of seventy, Craig sold the company to Toledo Shipbuilding in 1906, which later became American Shipbuilding.

Craig remained in Toledo the rest of his life, nearly thirty more years. He lived in a large home at 2105 Madison Avenue, and he used to walk the fifteen blocks to his office in the Nicholas Building with his banker friend C. C. Whitmore every day.

Later in his life, Craig liked to recall events

of his earlier days. He liked to recall his meetings with famous people such as the poet William Cullen Bryant, Henry Ward Beecher, and Peter Cooper, builder of the first locomotive.

He also remembered as a boy of 12 standing on a New York dock watching the old schooner-rigged yacht "America" sail off to win this country's first international race. His love for ships began at that early age. Years later, yachts owned by the Craig family won many races on the Great Lakes.

Craig was also involved in politics throughout his long life. The first vote he ever cast was for Abraham Lincoln in the 1860 presidential election. He was in the audience at New York's Cooper Institute on February 27, 1860, when Lincoln made his famous speech that helped turn the course of the election.

A life-long Republican, Craig surprisingly helped elect Toledo's best known independent mayor, Samuel "Golden Rule" Jones. Craig had been a candidate for mayor on the Republican ticket, but petty factional politics within the party caused him to throw his considerable support to Jones who was elected on the next ballot.

In 1908, Craig was even a candidate for nomination to be President of the United States. He agreed to have his name presented only on the condition that his supporters would cast their votes for William Howard Taft if Craig's nomination failed, as he knew it would. Of course, Taft was elected President that year.

During his business career, Craig held many important positions. He was president of the Toledo Steamship Company, Adams Transportation, and the Monroe Transportation Company, director of the First National Bank, and vice-president of the Toledo Metal Wheel Company. He also was on the board of

Flower Hospital, the Toledo Club, the Toledo Yacht Club, and a trustee of St. Paul's Methodist Church.

Captain Craig's wife, Annie Losee Craig, died in 1932, two weeks after they had celebrated their 71st wedding anniversary. It was the custom in their household to begin the holiday celebrations on November 4th, their anniversary, and conclude them on Christmas Day, the Captain's birthday. The Craigs had two sons and a daughter, and at the time of his death there were ten grandchildren and 10 great-grandchildren.

His obituary said "he found work a cure for worry and he never rusted from inaction." Captain John Craig was typical of those hardy individuals who brought the shipping industry to the Great Lakes. Like the boats he built, his busy and productive life allowed him little time to rust from inaction.

WARD'S CANAL RECALLS SHIPPING DAYS NEAR BONO

Lake Erie's southern shore was also once an important center for shipbuilding, with even a shipyard that employed about 100 men near what is the present-day town of Bono. But all that remains today of that thriving enterprise is the old canal still seen meandering along Route 2 by travelers on their way to Cedar Point.

A local farmer and businessman, Martin Z. Wiener, wrote a history of the once-prosperous shipyard and its access canal. The book recalls that for a short time during the 1870s this section of Jerusalem Township thirteen miles east of Toledo was a major shipbuilding center.

Dense forests of oak, maple, cedar, cotton-wood, and pine covered the township before the Civil War. Then, two years after the war ended, Detroit industrialist Captain Eber Brock Ward bought 8,500 acres of oak timber for shipping, but had no way to get the lumber out of the swampy area.

Captain Ward solved the problem by towing a steam dredge down from Detroit, and with the help of picks and shovels, dug a canal about two and a half miles from Cedar Creek to the lake. The canal was 30 feet wide, 15 feet deep, and ran east along Route 2 for less than a mile until turning northeast toward the lake.

Near the present intersection of Route 2 and Lyons Road, Captain Ward built a whole lumber town with a sawmill, boarding house for mill hands, horse stable, and race track. The town, which he named "New Jerusalem," no longer exists.

About one and a half miles east of the sawmill, Captain Ward built his shipyard on the north side of the canal. It prospered immediately, and at least four large schooner-barges were built there. But the prosperity proved to be short-lived. The economic panic of 1873 shut down the shipyard, and Captain Ward died two years later in Detroit. His elegant home was sold, the boarding house was divided into two homes, the sawmill was turned into an onion storehouse, and New Jerusalem became a memory.

Another town across from Ward's old shipyard was called Shephardsville. Two brothers named Shephard who operated a saloon and boarding house applied for a post office under that name, but were turned down because another Ohio town had already taken the Shephardsville name. Instead, they chose the name of a respected Indian, Joseph Bunno, which over time was shortened to Bono.

Other businesses were tried in the area. In 1880, Fred Tank built a stave mill near the former shipyard. But in 1895, a muck fire that lasted all summer destroyed most of the trees in the area, putting an end to the lumber industry. The region was then cleared, drained, diked, and farmed. The old canal was still used by small vessels to haul onions to other Lake Erie ports.

Today a barn on Mr. Wiener's farm stands on the foundations of the once-thriving shipyard. The shoreline of Jerusalem Township has become a nature preserve and residential area for boating enthusiasts. But Ward's Canal still serves as a reminder of the oak forests and shipbuilding industry that once thrived during the early days of Jerusalem Township.

EAST SIDE PHOTOGRAPHER RECORDED EARLY TOLEDO

Charles F. Mensing, who grew up in East Toledo, became interested in photography at the age of ten. For the rest of his life he continued to record the growth of the city and the pastimes of its inhabitants, especially the scenes of his childhood on the East Side.

His father, Herman R. Mensing, came to America from Germany in 1852. Herman and his wife Minnie opened a general store in 1878 at 1147 Miami Street near the corner of Fassett, a building still standing. Charles was born two years later, the eldest of three sons and a daughter.

The Miami-Fassett area is one of the oldest neighborhoods in East Toledo, platted in the 1850s. The Mensing's store served the interesting mix of immigrant families who settled there by the docks and railroads that supplied to the fast-growing city.

When the Fassett Street Bridge opened in the 1890s, the area prospered. Other stores, like Rodemich's at 1129 Miami Street and Olds' Grocery at Fassett and Utah, went into business. Industry flourished along the river. And Dr. Hathaway began his medical practice on the site of the old Indian fort at Miami and Fort Street (later renamed Hathaway Street). Lincoln School (also later called Hathaway) was built between Felt and Utah Streets. Also in the area, Dawson Chapel opened in 1873 and Clark Street Methodist in 1890 began to serve the religious needs of the community.

The young photographer was fascinated by the bustling life he saw all around him. Again and again he would climb down from his buggy to set up the heavy camera and tripod to capture people about their business or a merchant posed in front of a store. Once he climbed precariously to the top of the old Union Elevators at Miami and Navarre to get a photograph of sailing ships docked at the elevators across the river.

His father had become a member of the board of fire commissioners, and young Charles joined the department on January 5, 1899, at the age of 18. In 1903 he was appointed fire operator, and by 1927 he became assistant superintendent of the whole fire and police alarm system for the city.

However, even as his duties increased, Charles Mensing's interest in photography continued. He roamed all over Toledo to take his pictures, and was especially interested in photographing people enjoying their leisure time at Toledo's many new beautiful city parks.

Mensing was also interested in the city's progress, and he documented new construction, the harbor, the railroads, and the many prospering new neighborhoods. And over the years, he continued to return to the scenes of his childhood and photograph the changes a new generation brought to the old Miami-Fassett area.

Charles Mensing has left hundreds of photographs, most of which are in the local history collection at the Main Library downtown. He died in 1950, but his legacy lives on in the record he has preserved of the people and places of an earlier time in Toledo, especially the neighborhood of his East Side childhood.

Charles Mensing.

EAST SIDE BIKERS SET TRANSCONTINENTAL RECORD

At 9:15 on the morning of June 1, 1896, East Siders Norman DeVaux and John LaFrance left New York City in an attempt to break the transcontinental speed record for bicycles. DeVaux, only 19 years old, and LaFrance, not yet 23, wore the colors of the Toledo Wheeling Association, but neither cyclist had ever ridden on a long distance tour or even entered a race.

This was the height of the 1890s bicycle craze in Toledo when the city had 22 cycle manufacturers led by the Gendron Wheel Company, so all of East Toledo followed the two young bikers' progress closely.

At the time they left New York, they were trying to beat the best previous record time of 47 days, 19 hours. But in the meantime, Captain John H. Witts of the Fall River Cycle Club had just finished a run from San Francisco to New York in a new record of only 40 days, 22 hours, and 15 minutes. This put even more pressure on the Toledo bikers.

Each day during their trip the two young men posted a report on their progress. Remarkably, they did not have a single mechanical breakdown, and only a few punctures. They were given "flattering receptions" all along the way, and at Syracuse and Chicago "they were the lions of the hour." To show their trip was official, the bikers carried documents with the signature of the Mayor of New York City, and also added the signatures of dignitaries in the various cities they passed through.

J. J. DeVaux, Norman's father and East Side bicycle merchant, told the Toledo News-Bee he followed the progress of the riders from city to city, but during the last three or four days of the ride he lost contact with his son. He last heard from the bikers at Winnemucca, Nevada, over 200 miles from San Francisco.

To get a report, Mr. DeVaux wired to Chicago and to Humboldt, Nevada, asking about where his son was last seen. In all, he spent $15, a large sum at that time, on telegrams. Finally, a postmaster at Reno reported that the bikers were due to arrive there at any moment.

At last, at 8:30 PM on July 8th, DeVaux and LaFrance rode into San Francisco. The United Press wired that "two tired and dusty wheelmen rode up to the city hall and were immediately surrounded by a group of cyclists who had been waiting many hours in expectation of their coming." They had completed the record-breaking trip in exactly 37 days, 14 hours, and 30 minutes. On their journey they had crossed eleven states and covered a distance of 3,365 miles, nearly 100 miles a day.

The news "caused general rejoicing on the East Side, where the youngsters were favorably known," the News-Bee reported. Mr. DeVaux ran to his home at 656 Platt Street to break the news to his wife. Bulletins were posted along Main and Front Streets and in many of the businesses to celebrate the ride.

The automobile, however, soon would put an end to the bicycle craze of the 1890s. By 1907 Mr. DeVaux had to operate a bowling alley at 518 Main Street to keep his bicycle shop going. That same

year, Norman DeVaux left Toledo to live in San
Francisco.   Two years earlier, in 1905, John
LaFrance gave up his carpenter's job at the
shipyards and also moved away. But even though
the new automobiles easily broke all speed and
distance records of that era, the accomplishment of
these two young East Side bikers remains a
significant achievement today.

WILLIAM TUCKER: ADVOCATE FOR THE EAST SIDE

It would be difficult to think of any project to
improve the East Side during the early years of this
century that did not involve William H. Tucker.
Many of the landmarks and institutions that East
Toledoans now take for granted began in the Main
Street law offices of Mr. Tucker.

William Tucker came from an old American
family, many having served in the Revolutionary
War. His grandfather settled in Ohio before 1820,
and Mr. Tucker was born in Lorain County on
October 6, 1849, the son of a prominent physician.

After graduating from Baldwin University, he
studied at both Yale and Cornell. The new graduate
came to Toledo in 1874 to study law at the firm of
Haynes and Potter, and he was admitted to the bar
two years later. On April 10, 1884, he married
Harriet VanGorder, and they had six children.

Over the years, Mr. Tucker had several law
partners, including D. H. James, with whom many of
his plans to improve the East Side were hatched.
Mr. Tucker was also the founder and president of
the East Side Commercial Club.

William Tucker House, 516 Arden Place.

From 1894 to 1898, he was a member of the
school board, and helped strengthen the existing
elementary schools on the East Side or else build
new ones. East Side Central was built in 1895 under
his leadership on the board. Also, as president of
the board of trustees of the University of Toledo,
Mr. Tucker almost single-handedly kept that
institution afloat during its difficult early struggles.

In addition, he became a powerful figure in
the Republican Party of Northwest Ohio, serving as
committee chairman during several campaigns and
helping to elect fellow Ohioan William McKinley
President of the United States. His political power,
along with his role on various judicial and municipal
committees, put him in a position to influence the
city for the good of the East Side, which he did on
many occasions.

On January 11, 1899, President McKinley appointed him to the important position of Postmaster of Toledo. During his sixteen years with the Post Office, Mr. Tucker initiated many reforms, made the system more efficient, and built the imposing building on Madison Avenue that was the main office for many years. He is remembered as one of the best administrators in the history of the Toledo postal service.

Beyond all his other accomplishments, the building of Waite High School was perhaps Mr. Tucker's most significant achievement. Along with Irving Macomber, he was very influential in locating the high school on the East Side. Now, over 75 years later, Waite is still vital to the life of East Toledo, as well as being one of its outstanding landmarks.

After retiring from the Post Office, Mr. Tucker resumed his law practice at 310 Main Street. He continued working there until his death on January 12, 1921, at the age of 71. His home, though altered and at one time a funeral home, remains at 516 Arden Place and is still an outstanding example of Queen Anne architecture.

Although no street, building, or school is named for him, few East Siders had as much influence or did as much good for the community as did William H. Tucker.

CAPT. D.H. JAMES: ANOTHER TIRELESS EAST SIDER

Another name that keeps reappearing in the histories of important East Side projects is that of Captain Daniel H. James. Like his fellow attorney, William Tucker, Captain James seems to have been

involved in almost every civic improvement in East
Toledo during the first years of the 20th century.

A University of Michigan graduate, Captain
James located on the East Side as a young man in
1891, and opened a law office at 211 Main Street the
next year. It did not take him long to make his
presence felt in the community.

As a member of City Council he was
responsible for the opening of the Mott Avenue
district by providing a sewer sufficient for its
needs. His legal work paved the way, so to speak,
for the opening of many new streets and additions
during those years of East Toledo's rapid expansion.

Along with Mr. Tucker, who was his law
partner at the time, Captain James came up with the
idea for the first Waite High School athletic bowl. He
argued that Waite should take advantage of the
natural "amphitheater" in front of the school which
he compared to the stadiums of ancient Greece. Of
course, many important football games were indeed
played in the Waite Bowl, especially against arch-
rival Scott, before the current stadium was opened
in 1934, also making use of the natural ravine of the
old East Side swale.

As a member of the Board of Education,
Captain James was instrumental in arranging for the
construction of the new Franklin and Raymer schools
in 1924. His proposed building program secured for
East Toledo a large share of a bond issue during
that time. He also was an influential originator of
the movement to obtain the old Bank Lands, which in
the 1930s became Pearson Park.

One of his proposals was unfortunately never
realized.   It was Captain James who urged a
boulevard system for the East Side, with one scenic
boulevard to run from Navarre Park to Collins Park
and another to be developed out Starr Avenue all

the way to the Bank Lands. Neither was ever built.

His title of Captain was earned as inspector of rifle practice for the old Sixth Regiment, G.A.R., which later became the Sixteenth Regiment. According to George Pearson, Captain James also organized the first signal company in the state and was its first captain.

In addition, he served as captain of the Ford Post Cadets at the time of the Spanish-American War, and during World War I the military draft board met in his office. He organized a company of home guards during the war and usually served as the grand marshall of East Side patriotic parades as well.

An interesting event, indicative of that period, was recorded during Captain James' membership in the old Toledo Battery. A mock training battle was to be staged in the old Armory, using an early type of machine-gun. While handling the ammunition, Captain James noticed that the cartridges, of course supposed to be blanks, were unusually heavy. He immediately gave the order to hold fire. Loaded cartridges had been issued by mistake, and Captain James had halted the proceedings just before several people would certainly have been killed.

Many other civic projects were launched in his law offices. He helped organize the Toledo, Port Clinton and Lakeside inter-urban railroad line, and also the East Side Community YMCA. He still found time to prepare city and state legislation free of charge for persons desiring action in the City Council or state legislature, to work on many East Side legal problems, and to incorporate many East Side firms and businesses.

In 1916 Captain James moved his law offices to 218 Main Street, where he remained until his death in 1927. He residence was at 418 Starr Avenue from

1897 until 1912 when he moved to 554 Arden Place at the corner of Nevada. The large brick home, which later became a Christian Scientist Church, still stands, the only reminder of a dedicated East Sider who deserves to be better remembered today.

GAMBLERS BOMBED HOUSE OF EAST SIDE LAWYER IN 1936

At 4:18 AM, on April 15th, 1936, the Mark Winchester family was jolted awake by a bomb exploding outside their home. The blast blew a hole one foot in diameter in the foundation of the house at 816 Euclid Avenue, shattering several windows in the Winchester home and the other houses nearby. Fortunately, no one was injured in the explosion.

Mr. Winchester, another prominent East Side attorney, had recently won several damage claims, some of them for large amounts, against local gamblers. He expressed the belief that the bombing was an "intimidation threat." Any thought that the explosion was caused by a gas leak was dispelled when police found near the house several pieces of fuse from a homemade dynamite bomb.

Windows were broken in the homes of Councilman Frank Consaul (758 Euclid), William McGranahan, Harlan Diehr, Alton Baker (next door to the Winchesters), and E. F. Heydinger at 809 Euclid who called the police. The first police detectives to arrive on the scene were Captains Ralph Van Vorce and Arthur Beseske and Sergeant Glenn Berning. They were assisted by Patrolmen John O'Connell and Howard Wenland.

The only clue was provided by John Benner of 838 Euclid. He told the officers that four men driving an old black sedan approached his wife the day before and asked the location of the Winchester house. After she pointed it out, the men returned to their car and drove slowly past the house without stopping. Police believed the same men came back that night and threw the dynamite at the house. A twelve-inch fuse on the explosive gave them time to get away before the bomb went off.

The family members in the house at the time, in addition to Mr. Winchester, were his wife Constance, their son Bruce, and Mrs. Winchester's 75-year-old mother, Mrs. Ella Hall. Rushing out of the house, they could smell burning rubber and powder, and saw a cloud of smoke near the front porch. The other son, Eugene, who still maintains a law office in the Spitzer Building, and the daughter, Mary, were away at school at the time of the bombing.

The Winchesters have long been a well-known East Side family. Mr. Winchester graduated from Harvard Law School before starting his practice in Toledo, and Mrs. Winchester, who attended Raymer, East Side Central, and the University of Toledo, taught in East Side elementary schools. They were married in 1907, and were active at Eastminster Presbyterian where Mrs. Winchester often was church organist. Their three children all went to East Side Central, Waite High School, and Dennison University.

Four years before the bombing, a Toledo paper reported Mr. Winchester's success at "suing gamblers in common pleas court for the return of money lost at the gambling tables." He had already entered some thirty cases and in most of them had gained out of court settlements or restitution with damages.

The gamblers who bombed the Winchester home in 1936 were never caught, but their warning went unheeded. Mark Winchester continued his successful law career and campaign against illegal gambling interests, and the house at 816 Euclid is still standing as a reminder of this noteworthy and prominent East Side family who were not intimidated by those who scoffed at the law.

PROHIBITION DAYS AT LA TABERNILLA

La Tabernilla, mecca for thirsty Toledoans during the Prohibition era, has disappeared along with the bootleggers who made it famous. The fashionable supper club that stood at 5451 Bay Shore Road is gone but not forgotten. The mention of its name usually brings a wry smile and knowing look from older Toledoans who remember its notorious heyday. East Side historian Cal O. Gettings once recalled, "It was anything you could name. But it was never a church."

Built in 1917 at a cost of $64,000, the sprawling mansion was designed with the long horizontal lines, wide overhangs, and low-pitched roof of the prairie style made famous by Frank Lloyd Wright in the early years of the century. The legend that Wright himself designed it has never been substantiated. At any rate, the early patrons who visited the "Tab" had other things on their minds besides architecture.

The cool breeze coming off Maumee Bay along with the excellent food and bootleg liquor made it a very popular place during the 1920s and early 1930s. The first-floor bar provided a rendezvous for people to drink until the wee hours of the night. The doors were not closed as long as any paying customers were still on hand. The Latin motto in the chimney sums up the mood of the times: "While we live, let us live."

The upstairs was devoted to gambling. Thousands of dollars, a substantial amount in those days, would change hands at a single toss of the dice. There was also scandal and intrigue associated with La Tabernilla, as secret deals and schemes were plotted in those upstairs rooms. In 1931, several county officials and Toledo merchants were indicted in a jail food scandal that was planned at La Tabernilla. A frequent patron was Thomas "Yonnie" Licavoli, the gang leader who was said to have "muscled in" on the profits.

The first owner had refused to sell illicit bootleg liquor. He soon went broke. When the next owner had no such reservations, La Tabernilla became very profitable, and also began to establish its reputation. Precautions, however, were necessary. Telephone poles were sunk offshore in the bay to hold signal lanterns. The rum-runners

La Tabernilla, one week before it burned in 1984.

from Canada could see the warning signals with
their spyglasses and know whether or not it was
safe to come ashore. During renovations many years
later, those beacon lights were found.

With the end of Prohibition in the 1930s, La
Tabernilla began its decline. Licavoli was put in the
Ohio penitentiary and gambling was ended during
the relentless cleanup by Frazier Reams, the well-
known Lucas County prosecuting attorney, and by
lawyers like Mark Winchester.

The owners of La Tabernilla defaulted on a
$5,000 mortgage note to industrialist Benjamin
Hazelton. Hazelton, however, who was in poor
health, committed suicide by leaping from the ninth
floor of the Commodore Perry Hotel on February 3rd,
1940. Two public auctions in 1940 produced no
bidders for the property.

In a somewhat ironic historical twist, the
building was later sold to Richard and Ruth Remmert
who converted the 23-room mansion into the Bay
Shore Rest Home. It remained a nursing home for
many years, but gradually fell into further decline.

In 1976, Mrs. Remmert sold La Tabernilla to
Larry and Dee Palmerton who saved it from the
wrecking ball. They installed a modern kitchen and
restored the dining rooms overlooking the bay. For
several years it was used as a banquet hall for
weddings, proms, and meetings. By 1984, however,
the building was again vacant. On September 2nd
firefighters burned it down to make room for new
condominiums and a marina, one week after Mr.
Gettings took a picture of the decaying old building.

But the old night spot still lives in memory as
a symbol of an earlier era. Perhaps when boats
dock after dark at the new marina, the lights will
remind some people of the signal lanterns that once
guided the rum-runners ashore with that cargo

awaited by the ladies and gentlemen in evening dress in those upstairs rooms at La Tabernilla so many years ago.

EAST TOLEDO'S OLDEST FUNERAL HOME

Michael Hoeflinger, who came to America with his widowed mother at the age of 16, opened the first funeral home in East Toledo in 1877. When he arrived in Toledo, he already had a knowledge of cabinet-making and was able to get a job with the firm of Newhaus & Allen.

Cabinet-making translated easily into making coffins, and Mr. Hoeflinger soon had an undertaking business in the Platt Building at Front and Main (where McDonald's is today), and there he also continued to do cabinet work whenever he did not have a coffin to make.

On October 9th, 1877, Mr. Hoeflinger married Susanna Schneider and they had nine children. Agnes became Toledo's first licensed lady embalmer, and Theodore also followed into the family business. The funeral home at 201 Platt Street was built in 1900 and was in use for nearly 90 years.

Michael Hoeflinger was active in many East Side organizations, especially the life of Sacred Heart Church where he devoted much time and money into the building of the present structure. He passed away on March 28, 1922.

Theodore continued to run the mortuary after his father's death. He was seriously injured in World War I at the battle of the Argonne forest and nearly bled to death on the field. He recovered, however, and lived to the age of 94. Today the

Hoeflinger's at Second & Platt, early 1900s.

business still flourishes and remains in the family under Michael A. Hoeflinger. A new funeral home has been opened at 3500 Navarre Avenue. East Toledo's first funeral business, 116 years later, is still doing well.

MORTICIAN RACED HORSES ON THE RIVER ICE

Whenever there was thick ice on the Maumee River, George M. Parks, East Side undertaker, would recall his racing days back at the turn of the century. Sometimes as many as 10,000 people would gather on the shore to watch the well-known trotters race on the Maumee River ice.

A one-half mile course was laid out that started by the old Ohio Central docks and extended to the Cherry Street Bridge. The drivers rode racing cutters, and the horses were shod especially for ice racing with "calks" in front and rear to prevent their feet from slipping forward or sideways. Mr. Parks' favorite horse was named "Billy Mason," and it was claimed that the trotter could go faster on the ice than on the streets.

One time tragedy almost struck. Mr. Parks was using his old ambulance horse, George, to haul planks down to the river and make a bridge so that horses from the West Side could get down to the ice. Suddenly he heard a warning shout.

The exhaust pipe from the old powerhouse on Water Street had melted the ice, and Mr. Parks didn't realize the danger until it was almost too late. He was able to turn back toward the East Side just in time to keep his horse, wagon, and himself from going into the river.

Many prominent Toledoans of that time, including George Ketchum, John Jackman, General Isaac Sherwood, Ed Mitchell, Herbert Chittenden, and several others enjoyed racing their horses on the river. When the ice was not thick enough, they held races on the snow-covered city streets. They raced on lower Superior Street and on Jefferson and Madison Avenues, with police patrolling to prevent accidents. Before the automobile put an end to street racing, the last races were held on Franklin Avenue from Cherry to Seventeenth Street.

Mr. Parks' most famous trotter was a horse called Eugene C, who was entered in races as far away as Cleveland. This horse suffered an unusual fate, caused by a woman with a trick horse who often entertained the crowds before a race. During one of its stunts, the woman's horse accidentally kicked a hole in the race track. Eugene C broke his leg by stepping in the hole and had to be put to sleep.

In addition to horse racing, Mr. Parks was a noted sportsman in other respects. He was an outstanding marksman, and once defeated the famous Annie Oakley in a shooting contest. When a Wild West show came to Toledo in 1887, he was one of two men chosen for the competition. Glass balls were tossed into the air, and Mr. Parks was able to hit more of the targets than Miss Oakley. This was his introduction to trapshooting, which he enjoyed until his 80th birthday. He was also a bicycle-racing enthusiast who competed in events in several cities, occasionally against fellow Toledoan, Barney Oldfield.

Mr. Parks was born in Perrysburg and raised on a farm where his father bred race horses. By the time he was eight years old, he was putting the horses through their paces on the mile-long course. He came to Toledo at the age of twelve and got a job driving the horses that pulled the railroad cars up to the old Wabash grain elevators. After owning a livery business, he became a mortician in 1888.

Mr. Parks was the first undertaker in the city to operate an ambulance service. He started with horse-drawn equipment and then later introduced the first motorized vehicles. He is also credited with having the first telephone installed in East Toledo.

His active life did not weaken his strong constitution. He remained a funeral director for 67 years, and died peacefully in his home in 1955 at the age of 91. And even in his last years, Mr. Parks recalled fondly those early days of racing horses whenever the ice grew thick on the Maumee River.

JAMES R. CLEGG: A MORTICIAN WHO SAVED LIVES

Although he was a member of the well-known East Toledo family of undertakers, James R. Clegg oddly enough became nationally recognized for his ability to save lives.

Before penicillin was widely used, Mr. Clegg was one of the few people to survive an infection of streptococcus veridans, which made him an effective blood donor for others who contracted the often deadly disease. During the remainder of his life, he traveled thousands of miles to provide blood transfusions for dying patients, and he is credited with saving at least fourteen lives.

Mr. Clegg was the son of Richard S. Clegg, who moved his undertaking business from Perrysburg to East Toledo in the 1890s. This hardy old pioneer, born in England, was a master woodworker who built boats, houses, and even his own solid black walnut casket. He ran the family business at 910 Starr Avenue until his death in 1930 when he was nearly ninety. Two of his sons, James and Worth W. Clegg, became morticians, and his daughter Anna married Howard Eggleston who was also an undertaker.

James Clegg was born in 1880 and grew up in Perrysburg. As a boy, he once delivered the Perrysburg Journal to General William McKinley, who was stationed there with the 16th Ohio Regiment. Mr. Clegg later served with that regiment during the Spanish-American War. After deciding to become a

mortician, he graduated from the Carl Barnes School
of Embalming and went to work for his father. The
Clegg Funeral Home, featuring an early motor-driven
ambulance and hearse, prospered during the early
years of this century.

In 1935, Mr. Clegg came down with the
dreaded streptococcus infection. He recovered after
a long siege, amazing even his own physician. Not
long after this, a call went out for emergency blood
donors to help an East Side mother who was ill at
Mercy Hospital. Mr. Clegg volunteered his fleet of
automobiles to take donors to the hospital. He did
not intend to donate blood himself, but he felt
foolish just standing there, so he got in line with
the other donors.

James Clegg seated on running-board, c. 1920.

After the blood of each donor was tested, an intern approached him and said a young boy in Windsor desperately needed his rare Moss Type IV blood. The boy was suffering from streptococcus veridans. His only hope was a transfusion from someone who had once had the disease. The next morning Mr. Clegg was on his way to Windsor.

The publicity that followed this humanitarian action led to many other similar requests, and Mr. Clegg honored as many as he possibly could, often traveling as far away as Baltimore or New York. Each transfusion required over a pint of his blood. He never asked for any compensation, and in most cases bore the cost of all travel expenses himself. He compiled a scrapbook full of clippings and grateful letters from people he helped, which the family has now donated to the East Toledo Historical Society.

Even though the transfusions were not always successful in saving a life, Mr. Clegg unselfishly continued to make trip after trip to donate his blood. By the time of his own death in 1948, he was responsible for saving the lives of at least fourteen people who otherwise would have prematurely needed the services of one of his fellow morticians.

HISTORY OF THE BERRY-PICKERS CLUB

For 28 years the "Berry-Pickers" had a clubhouse at 842 Butler Street in East Toledo. The two-story frame structure was built by neighborhood boys who earned the necessary money by picking in the berry patches of the small farms nearby. Built in 1900, the surprisingly sophisticated clubhouse stood until its second generation of young bachelors succumbed to the temptations of marriage.

The original members of the club were Alfred Matthews, L. J. Gaertner, Carl Matthews, George Bauer, and Adolph Gaertner (who was the president). They were given use of the property on Butler Street to build their clubhouse, and the group flourished for twelve years. The Berry-Pickers baseball team is still remembered by old timers as "one of the crack nines in amateur baseball circles of that time."

As older members married and left the club, a new generation was gradually taken into the Berry-Pickers. Other members during those early years were Paul Treter, James Skahill, Rudy Treter, Frank Billinsky, and W. J. Treter. In 1912, the group was re-incorporated as "Our Club," and the lot and clubhouse were purchased by Carl Matthews.

Berry-Pickers Clubhouse, circa 1918.

Several of the "Berry-Pickers" or "Our Club" members served in World War I. Some old pictures survive of members standing in front of the clubhouse in their military uniforms. They had just returned from France where they had fought with the Allied Expeditionary Forces.

Gradually, during the 1920's, this second generation of Berry-Pickers had their ranks depleted through death and marriage. By 1928, only two bachelors remained. And one of them, Edward Lindner, according to a history written by Harold Siewert, was already "feeling the call of the famous wedding march."

The other unmarried member when the clubhouse was finally torn down in 1928 was Otto Hoffman. He was called "official" by the boys, who described him as "a confirmed, uncompromising bachelor." They were greatly mistaken, however, and it was from his widow, Esther Hoffman, that much of this information about the club was provided.

Some of the activities inside the clubhouse consisted of card playing, meetings, and "socials." The young men would come dressed in coats and ties to a room furnished simply with spindle chairs and a spittoon. Only on special occasions would young ladies be invited inside.

One such occasion occurred in 1921. It concerned the last surviving member of the "Berry-Pickers", Edmund Matthews, who died in 1983 in his 88th year. Edna Matthews, his widow, has several pictures of the old clubhouse, and she clearly remembers the only time she was invited inside-- February 21, 1921. It was there on that day she met her husband, which seems a fitting way for the story of the young bachelors and their "Berry Pickers" clubhouse to end.

ANTICS OF THE SNOWBALL CLUB IN EARLY EAST TOLEDO

Not many Toledoans still remember the "boys" of the Snowball Club. In the early years of this century, Chris Rantz' barber shop was the usual gathering place for this group of boisterous East Toledo businessmen. When the little shop at the corner of Second and Main was torn down in the 1930's, George Pearson took the occasion to recall some of the Snowball Club's most notorious jokes, pranks, and antics.

Many of the leading merchants of the day were members of the Club, including the Munch brothers, Frank Lavoy, Chester Schultz, Ed Hulce, Gus Hoeflinger, Frank Muntz, Captain D. H. James, and George Parks. Sometimes they met at the Arlington Hotel across Second Street, but most often their "headquarters" was Rantz' one-story frame barber shop originally used by Dr. Seth Beckwith when he served as coroner.

The Snowball Club, however, was much more lively than a coroner's office, and as Pearson states, the "day was counted lost when some good joke was not worked out." It seems that not many days were counted lost.

One of the best remembered pranks perpetrated on this corner was the "telescopic view of Halley's Comet." When the famous comet appeared in 1909, Rantz obtained a small telescope and placed it on a tripod outside his shop for the curious to see the "wonders of science and the marvel of the universe." When darkness came, he would train his telescope at an angle along Main Street, pointing it at a "breaker" in the overhead trolley line. Whenever a streetcar passed over the jumper, there was always a bright flash greatly magnified by the telescope.

The innocent observer lined up at the telescope would see nothing at first, but he would see plenty when the streetcar jumped the circuit over the breaker. Some people were frightened by this mysterious light from the comet, and few ever knew at the time what caused this brilliant "display in the sky."

The success of this trick led to another prank involving the same telescope. On occasion Rantz would focus it on the full moon. First, however, he would put cockroaches, flies, or mosquitoes inside one of the lenses, treating observers to creatures they never imagined lived on the surface of the moon.

On slow days, reporters would pass the time with members of the Club: thus the story of The Black Panther of Bono. After an account of a murdered child in California appeared in the papers four straight days, Rantz decided to give a reporter something else to write about. He made up a story that a panther or huge wildcat had appeared between Reno Beach and Bono. It had probably come across the ice from Canada, Rantz stated, or else around the lake from the Michigan woods.

After the story appeared in the newspaper, the entire region from Reno Beach down into Ottawa County was up in arms, and a posse was organized to hunt the vicious animal. Several calves and sheep were reported as victims, and some people claimed to have actually seen the animal skulking through the dark woods and swamp grasses near Bono.

Perhaps the most amusing story of the Snowball Club involved the proprietor of the Arlington Hotel, Joseph Munch, and his amazing "money-making machine." The machine had small rollers, into which a blank piece of paper could be inserted. When a crank was turned, the blank paper would be folded under a cloth belt and a new crisp bank note would appear. The machine needed to be loaded with real money of course, but as Pearson writes, "the effect was startling."

Munch took this device to a bank where he was known. He placed the machine in front of a teller, put in a blank piece of paper, and produced a new $20 bill. He then asked the teller for change, which the teller indignantly refused to give. Munch then visited several other banks in the area.

The Arlington Hotel at Second & Main.

The next day a stranger arrived at the hotel to see this "counterfeiting device." Even though Munch knew the man was a government official, he could not resist demonstrating "how easy it was to make money," and offered to go 50-50 with the man. The agent exploded, "You can't trifle with me that way. You're under arrest!" Munch then showed him how the machine worked and they repaired, so the story goes, to the hotel bar and set up a round of drinks for the crowd.

Old photographs of early East Side businessmen often look so sober. It is refreshing to think of them in their lighter moments, and when going past the intersection of Second & Main Streets, perhaps recall some of the more outrageous antics of Chris Rantz and the members of the Snowball Club.

MOTHER & DAUGHTER HAVE 50th ANNIVERSARY SAME DAY

Old newspaper articles often reveal interesting items about the lives of East Siders who have now been forgotten. One very unusual item was a mother and her daughter who celebrated their golden wedding anniversaries on the same day: April 19, 1933. Such an event was so rare that it was recorded a few years later in Ripley's "Believe-It-Or-Not."

Julia Evelyn Fields, the mother who shared this unique experience with her daughter, Evelyn Long, came from the oldest East Side family. She was the last of 17 children born to Robert and Catherine Navarre, members of the pioneer family who were the first settlers east of the river in 1807.

Julia Fields' unusual marital circumstances

came about in the following manner: Her first
husband, Evelyn's father, died shortly after the
birth of his daughter. Julia was only eighteen years
old at the time. Years later, she married her second
husband, Edward Fields, on the same day that her
daughter was wed to George Long of Rossford. The
marriages took place on the East Side in 1883, and
the Fields later left the Robert Navarre farmlands
out Manhattan Avenue to move back to 1650 Oak
Street in East Toledo.

The couples were blessed with extreme
longevity. Both husbands and wives were still alive
when the 50th anniversary of the double wedding
rolled around. On that occasion, the Pioneer Club of
Edison Review gave a huge party in their honor at
the lodge hall at Sixth & Main Streets, just a few
blocks from where the Longs were married 50 years
before.

Shortly afterwards, the Fields and Longs came
to the attention of Robert L. Ripley, who wrote the
famous   "Believe–It–Or–Not"   articles   in   the
newspapers. In March 1937, their story appeared in
papers all around the country, as well as on Ripley's
national radio program, while the two couples were
preparing   to   celebrate   their   54th   wedding
anniversaries together.

Edward Fields passed away in September 1939,
and Julia Fields followed in November 1940 at the
age of ninety. At the time of her death, she left
four children in addition to Mrs. Long, thirteen
grandchildren, nineteen great-grandchildren, and
fifteen great-great-grandchildren. The unusual tale
of these two couples is just one of the many
interesting   local   stories   that   should   not   be
forgotten.

TOLEDO WRITER REMEMBERS HER EAST SIDE CHILDHOOD

Dale Fife, author of <u>Weddings in the Family</u>, <u>The Unmarried Sisters</u>, and over twenty books for children, follows the practice of all good writers: she writes about what she knows best. For this reason, her books are about her love for nature, places she has lived or visited, and especially about her childhood memories of growing up in East Toledo.

Mrs. Fife's maiden name was Odile Hollerbach ("Dale" was an early nickname), and her family came from the German speaking French province of Alsace-Lorraine, though her father was a German from Baden. She was born in Ironville, but soon moved to the large stone house her parents built on the corner of Parker and Kelsey about 1904.

Many of the places mentioned in her popular novel <u>Weddings in the Family</u> are familiar to East Siders. Her childhood home described in the book had a view of the "Hollow" (now the Waite bowl and stadium), Sacred Heart Church, and the parish school where she attended, all still well-known landmarks today. Other familiar places, such as Starr Avenue and Von Ewegen's (Von Essen's) Drug Store, also appear.

The family in the book is named Houck, but the Hollerbach family is slyly mentioned near the end of the novel, as are the Ehrets, her mother's family name. "Odile" is the sister of the fictional narrator Shatzie.

In her letters, Mrs. Fife has recalled some of her childhood memories of East Toledo. She remembers "serious faced Mr. Von Ewegen who diagnosed our ailments," such as her father Herman's "bad dose of giant hives" which also appear in Weddings in the Family. She also recalls that the family did most of their shopping at Gross's (later J. C. Penney's) at First and Main. And she got her first automobile ride at the age of eight from a saloon keeper at the corner of Starr and East Broadway.

Her father worked six days a week as a foreman at the Wheeling Shops. As their foreman, he cared about the men in his "gang." Mrs. Fife remembers that "often on Sundays he would visit them--a Hungarian who had been injured in the shop; a Pole who needed help with his citizenship papers; a Bulgarian family having landlord trouble." Sometimes he took her with him, and she would notice the "husky boys" gathered on the street corners of Birmingham who would later become football players at Waite. Scott players called them "Boilermakers" because their fathers worked in the pig-iron mills.

She recalls her fascination with the people she saw on streetcar trips through Birmingham to Ironville. "The Hungarian women wore babushkas on their heads and colorful shawls over their shoulders. The Polish had a love affair with color: purples, reds, pinks." German women were more conservative, wearing "black skirts, white shirtwaists." In those days, houses were "coal mottled," and Mrs. Fife remembers "the blast furnaces of the area lighting up the night skies." The engineers on the Wheeling & Lake Erie Railroad used to wave to her as the train passed next to her aunt's house.

The house on Parker, however, was not close to the tracks, and the family (there were 32 first cousins in Toledo) had picnics in the nearby Pickle Woods. Her family spoke English at home; and whenever a relative came to America from the "other side," the first thing Mr. Hollerbach did was to take the new arrival to night school to learn American ways. Mrs. Fife learned her German at Sacred Heart School. As immigrants, the family was occasionally referred to as "Greenhorns."

Food always plays a part in childhood memories. When Mrs. Fife's father paid the week's grocery bill at Gross's on Saturday night, he would bring home a "treat," usually a bag of mixed candy. There was a nearby bakery that had big, crunchy "sugar cookies" for 5 cents, and Von Ewegen's was a "treasure house" of penny candy and lacy valentines. Occasionally the family crossed the Cherry Street Bridge to get their sausages at Kurtz' Market on Summit Street.

Mrs. Fife finished her education and has lived most of her life in California where she is currently writing Go West about her years spent in Nevada. A few years ago she returned to northwest Ohio to visit the scenes of her childhood, especially a woods near Norwalk still as beautiful as she remembered it when she was seven, and her book The Empty Lot is based on that experience.

By preserving her memories through her gift for storytelling, Mrs. Fife has also preserved a feeling for the day-to-day lives of real people when she was a young girl growing up in East Toledo.

GEORGE PEARSON: EAST SIDE REPORTER FOR 52 YEARS

A tribute to George Pearson reads: "He made the East Side not only his beat, but his life's work."

Mr. Pearson, who reported on the people and events of East Toledo for fifty-two years, became known as "the first citizen of the East Side."

Born in 1870 in Covington, Ohio, Mr. Pearson showed his early interest in journalism by working as a Blade correspondent while he was still a high school senior in Van Wert. After two years at Ohio Wesleyan University, where he was the top student in his class, Mr. Pearson taught in a country school near Grover Hill for $40 a month.

He then worked for a year at a Solar Refinery while taking classes at Lima Business College in the evenings. Returning to Van Wert, he went to work on the railroad, but spent most of his free time setting type and reporting for the Daily Bulletin, simply because he enjoyed the work.

George Pearson House, 515 St. Louis, built 1901.

When he arrived in Toledo in 1893, Mr. Pearson was hired as a reporter at the old Toledo News for $6 a week. Three months later he switched to The Blade where he remained until his retirement in 1947. During that time a special column was created for him so that he could report on "his beloved East Side."

For over half a century Mr. Pearson covered sports, business, social events, fires, police stories, church and school news, and any other story of note about those living east of the river. He accompanied Edward Ford when he laid out the first glass plant in Rossford at the turn of the century. He reported the construction of the Toledo Furnace factory that became Interlake Iron, and also the building of the initial Standard Oil refinery.

It was in Mr. Pearson's East Side column that the demand for the paving of Front Street was first made. When that was accomplished, he began a campaign that resulted in the building of Waite High School on the East Side. He promoted and championed the widening of Main Street, the building of the Hi-Level Bridge, and the formation of an East Side branch of the YMCA. He took two years off work from 1920-22 to serve as the East Side YMCA's first director.

Known as "a one-man Chamber of Commerce," he helped John Gunckel with his Old Newsboys Association, served nineteen years on the Toledo Public Library Board, and was a member of the board of the Toledo Council of Churches. He was a Sunday School teacher and superintendent at Second Congregational Church on Fourth Street for twenty-five years. He organized dozens of service clubs and benefit programs, and promoted any other activity to make Toledo a better place to live.

But perhaps his best known campaign was his effort to save the Bank Lands, over 300 acres of

virgin timber which he thought would make an
excellent East Side park. Through his column, Mr.
Pearson was able to convince some businessmen to
help the Park Commission purchase the land before
the trees were all chopped down.   The land was
saved.   On August 30th, 1934, the park was
dedicated, and today Pearson Metropark attracts
thousands of visitors a year. Only reluctantly did
Mr. Pearson let grateful citizens name the park in
his honor.

An associate of Mr. Pearson's at The Blade for
over forty-five years said, "I never heard him speak
a mean or ignoble word; I never knew him to do a
mean or ignoble thing." At his retirement, he said
he tried to live by the philosophy: "What the world
needs is not more education, not more wealth, but a
kind heart." In his papers is a letter from Theodore
Roosevelt commending Mr. Pearson for his
"principles," saying they "are just exactly those for
which I should like to feel that I stand."

Mr. Pearson had married Blanche Diggery on
March 24, 1895, and they enjoyed fifty-six years
together until her death in 1951 at the age of 78.
They had two sons: Kenneth and Eugene. In 1901,
Mr. Pearson built a house at 515 St. Louis, where he
lived the rest of his life. He died at home after a
long illness in 1955.

Anyone who has read his columns and articles
can appreciate his informative, lively writing. But
more importantly, he has preserved the memory of
countless events and people who would otherwise be
forgotten, and also has promoted so many civic
projects that have made the East Side a better place
to live.   One of his colleagues put it best:
"Everywhere we see monuments to George Pearson,
living monuments--the lives of all the men and
women he influenced and helped."

Chapter   9

EAST SIDE, EAST SIDE, ALL AROUND THE TOWN...

*

Other Attractions East of the River

from

The Building of Historic Homes

to

The End of the Streetcar Era

*

EAST SIDE HOMES FEATURE A VARIETY OF ARCHITECTURE

An important feature of the East Side is that
it has retained most of its original housing stock,
which includes a wide variety of architectural
styles. This is one reason that four areas of East
Toledo are being considered for historic designation
on the list of the National Register of Historic Places.

Many fine examples of architecturally
significant homes can be found on the East Side.
During the boom years of the 1880s and 1890s,
prosperous merchants, oil drillers, industrialists,

and professionals built large homes especially in the Victorian Hilltop area at the upper end of Euclid Avenue and south of Starr Avenue between Main Street and St. Louis. Often these imposing homes share the same streets as earlier farm houses and uniform-plan developments. An imposing Queen Anne often sits next to modest workers' cottages.

Queen Anne houses were the most popular design of the late Victorian period, with most of them being built in the 1890s. The B. R. Baker home on Parker near Starr Avenue is a particularly good example. It has the cross-gabled hipped roof that distinguishes Queen Anne houses, but also features a two-story bay window and diamond windowed gables with shingle detailing. Other vintage Queen Anne homes are the William Tucker house (with a fine turret, but unfortunately covered with siding) at 516 Arden Place, the Bihl house (complete with carriage house behind) at Greenwood and St. Louis,

Bihl House, Greenwood & St. Louis, about 1915.

and the huge Wolf mansion at Greenwood and Arden Place.

Many Neo-classical houses with their imposing two-story front pillars can be found on East Toledo streets. For example, there is the former Eggleston-Meinert Funeral Home on Main Street with its particularly fine classical facade. The Elijah Woodruff house on Garfield Place behind the Professional Building is another Neo-classical home which was built as early as 1852. A house with beautiful classical pillars can be found on Essex Street near Waite High School.

Farm houses often sit nestled between much later dwellings. At 1522 East Broadway a brick farm house of 1870 or earlier is found behind a newer home. A house left sitting behind later houses is an interesting East Side development. In other neighborhoods, the original house would not have been preserved. Another early farm house is the Crawford home at 814 Willow. Built in 1877, it is the oldest house in an area developed after the turn of the century.

A particularly charming aspect of East Side architecture is the number of quaint Folk Victorian houses with their extensive spindle-work and other early craftsman details. Two excellent examples are at 660 Platt Street and 1104 Greenwood. The home on Greenwood was built by a carpenter named Caspar Rohner, and its original fine details from the early 1870s have been well preserved.

Many other examples could be mentioned. Birmingham has some unique brick homes with double-arched porches, a design probably brought from the old world. The distinctive pre-cast concrete houses of the Spring Grove and Greenwood area were also made into row houses, such as the one at Fourth and Steadman. The Kesting house on East Broadway at Mott is an outstanding example of

Richardson Romanesque, and also has probably the largest carriage house on the East Side.

At the very least, historic designation would add to pride on the East Side, and perhaps also make residents more aware of the rich variety of architecture that still exists on almost every street.

EARLY NEIGHBORHOOD THEATERS OF THE EAST SIDE

Long before movie-goers were clustered into shopping malls, and long before the invention of the VCR, many now-forgotten theaters catered to the East Side's various neighborhoods. Most long-time East Toledoans can remember the East Auditorium and the Tivoli, both of which closed over thirty years ago, but few can recall such names as the Crescent, the Ideal, the Oak, or the Palm. They were just a few of the many theaters that once dotted the neighborhoods of East Toledo.

In the year 1911, four small East Side theaters appeared in city directories for the first time. "Amusements" were offered at the Crescent (930 Woodville Road), which survived only until 1917; the Palm (220 Paine), which lasted until 1931; the Navarre (at Oak and Navarre) which was in business until 1923; and the Peoples Theater (at 804 Starr Avenue).

These theaters provided various types of entertainment and catered mainly to their immediate vicinities. Several other small theaters also opened in the early teens: the Ideal at 306 Fassett Street, the Oak at 509 Oak Street, and the Gaiety at 2156 Front Street. Not one of these was able to outlast the first World War.

In addition, in those early years, the Alvin or New Palace Theater presented Vaudeville performers in the Weber Block, and the Gem Theater entertained East Siders in the Montville Block at the corner of First and Main. The most successful of the early theaters, however, were the East Auditorium and for a short time the Japanese Garden.

On Christmas Day of 1913, A. J. Smith and his son Martin opened the East Auditorium at 519 Main Street, so that "the people of East Toledo could enjoy the popular movies at a price that was reasonable." The motion picture industry was just beginning and the East Auditorium brought these popular "photo plays" to the East Side. On June 6, 1915, for example, movie-goers could see "The Castle Ranch" or "Love and Sour Notes" on the East Auditorium's big screen.

Garden Theater, 1914-20, now site of Huntington Bank.

In 1914, Mr. Smith joined with James A. Beidler, who had been operating the Peoples Theater next to the fire station at the corner of Starr and Main since 1911. After expensive remodeling, they reopened the Peoples as the Japanese Garden Theater, which they operated in addition to their East Auditorium. The Japanese Garden was the first outdoor theater in Toledo, long before Drive-ins became popular in the late 1930s. It was perhaps ahead of its time, however, and it closed in 1920 never to be reopened.

The Smith and Beidler theaters were known for family entertainment. They sought to provide "clean, high-class entertainment, booking only the best shows, where parents could safely take or send their children." The success of the East Auditorium led to the opening of a similar theater, the Eastwood. It opened in 1921 and was also successful in attracting neighborhood families.

The neighborhood theaters were "subsequent run" houses, showing movies several weeks or months after the large downtown theaters, but that did not seem to hurt their business. And what a bargain they were. First there was an episode of a continuing serial, then newsreels, one or more cartoons, a short western, two or three comedies, and finally a feature picture--all for one dime!

Harold Lloyd, Buster Keaton, or Charlie Chaplin perhaps appeared in the featured comedies, Tom Mix, Ken Maynard, or Hoot Gibson might be in the western, or maybe there was a horror-thriller with Lon Chaney or Boris Karloff. In September of 1926, Harold Lloyd in "For Heaven's Sake" was at the East Auditorium, and the Eastwood was featuring William Boyd in "Volga Boatman."

The coming of the "talkies" only added to the popularity of the movies, and the Eastwood and East Auditorium continued to flourish. On March 2, 1942,

"They Died with their Boots On" was at the Eastwood, starring Errol Flynn. A movie-goer on July 22, 1944, could choose between "Once Upon a Time" with Cary Grant at the Eastwood, or Paulette Goddard in "The Lady Has Plans" at the East Auditorium.

The theaters also held drawings. A lucky ticket holder might win a free ham or box of candy, depending on the night of the week. These were valuable prizes during the Depression years. The 1950s saw the weekly Bank Nights, an early version of today's lotteries. In addition to the movies, East Siders were offered other forms of entertainment at some establishments. The New Miami Inn at 1401 Miami Street featured live nightly performers such as "Helene: The Girl with the Radio Mind" and "Alva Vincent, Exponent of Tease."

The coming of television began the decline of the neighborhood theater. Today the Eastwood is the only East Side theater still in operation. Mr. Smith passed away in 1926 and his son carried on the East Auditorium until the 1950s. The Tivoli on Consaul Street, which opened in 1928, also went out of business during the 1950s.

Many of the old buildings still remain and have become part of other businesses. The East Auditorium later became a Pentecostal Church and it still stands next to the Coad Building at Sixth and Main. The Oak Theater is now part of Ondrus Hardware, the Navarre became Walter's Pharmacy, and the Palm is now the meeting place of the Hungarian Club. These surviving old buildings are a reminder of an earlier era when theaters were once as numerous as video stores in the neighborhoods of East Toledo.

THE FAMILY CENTER'S LONG EAST SIDE HISTORY

The East Toledo Family Center was the first institution of its kind in Toledo, and began serving the East Side in 1901.   Tim Yenrick, the current director, and Roger Dodsworth have brought to light several interesting letters and manuscripts that record the early history of the Center.

On Sunday, August 4th, 1901, Reverend H. W. Hoover, former Pastor of Memorial Baptist Church, held a tent mission on factory grounds owned by D. J. Nysewander at East Broadway and the NYC tracks. A list survives of those who contributed toward the "interest on loan, sidewalks, hymn books, lights, and piano-tuning" for this Industrial Heights Mission. Contributors included such well-known East Side names as Metzger, Rideout, Tracy, and Hirzel.

The Mission lasted for several days, and then was enlarged into "settlement work" to help the many new immigrants in the area become adjusted to life in America. By the summer of 1902 property was obtained on Vinal Street, and adjoining lots were soon added through the generosity of Alexander Black, George Metzger, Isaac Gerson, and Mr. Nysewander. Reverend Hoover and his wife Nellie moved into a large shed on the grounds until more permanent housing could be built.

The land, which was originally a neglected dump, was quickly improved. Dirt from the streets was used as fill, grass was sown, East Side florists provided flowers, the Monroe Nurseries gave shrubs, and the old dump became a thing of the past. The Ohio Neighborhood Institute, commonly called the Neighborhood House, was incorporated, and the property at 1019 and 1027 Vinal developed rapidly. M. J. Riggs, superintendent of the American Bridge Company, helped purchase playground equipment and also provided paint, fencing, and ornamental gates and posts.

An economic depression in 1908 led to what immigrant families in the area called the "slim winter." When no other charities were available to help the many families who were out of work, Mrs. Hoover and East Side businessmen stepped in to provide food and aid through the Neighborhood House.

In those early years before Oakdale was built, a school was held for a time at the Neighborhood House. Classes in English were also taught to both children and adults who had recently arrived in this country to work in the nearby factories. Another playground was established for the children at Ironville, and the bandstand formerly at Presque Isle was brought there. In 1921, Reverend Hoover purchased a cottage at Put-in-Bay, which enabled volunteer workers and immigrant families to enjoy a vacation they otherwise could not have afforded.

By 1927 the facilities at the Neighborhood House included the residence of the Hoovers, a care-taker's cottage, and an enlarged building that included an auditorium, kitchen, music room, and classroom space. Jewish families contributed toward the park that now had an improved playground and a new tennis court.

An early article proclaims the benefits of the Neighborhood House of that time. Because of its recreational programs, the article states, "the number of boys loitering on street corners" had noticeably decreased. The Neighborhood House had given them "a means to stay away from the pool halls," and through physical exercise made them "cleaner of mind and sounder of body."

The community programs and support offered by the Neighborhood House were perhaps never so valuable as during the years of the Depression. A letter from the 1930s vividly describes the "silent factory whistles," the "rags and tears," and the "discouragement" of those forced to be idle. The Neighborhood House helped pay utility bills, provided clothing and food, and offered free community entertainment programs to bolster peoples' spirits.

After seventy years at the Vinal Street location, the Neighborhood House needed larger facilities for all its programs. It moved a half mile down East Broadway to its present site at the corner of Varland, and the lease for the newly-named East Toledo Family Center was signed on September 9, 1971.

More programs are being offered at the Family Center than ever before. The Center provides recreational programs, meeting rooms for Scouts and clubs, health care programs, pre-school and Head Start, arts and crafts, hot noon meals for school children, the Senior Center at Navarre Park, and many other programs that have benefitted area residents. Through the years, from its humble beginnings in a mission tent, the East Toledo Family Center has served East Siders well.

STATION A: DELIVERING THE MAIL SINCE 1895

Postal Station A on the East Side was the first branch office to be established in Toledo, opening its doors on January 10, 1895. In those early days it distributed mail to about 12,000 residents living east of the river. Fifty years later, the same station was serving over four times as many patrons, nearly 55,000, and today it has grown even more.

Station A was first located in a storeroom of the Weber Block at the corner of Front and Main. It soon moved to an office at 502 Main Street where it remained for many years. Albert Eppstein was the first superintendent, and his clerk was Charles A. Kirk. The station opened with a staff of six carriers: John Waterbury, Harry Rake, Charles Hicks, Joseph Bihl, Charles Mayne, and George Humberstone. A seventh carrier, soon added, was Charles Reuscher.

Before the turn of the century, much of East Toledo was still orchards and farmland, making delivery of mail difficult in inclement weather. In 1896, a year after the station opened, a rural route was established. The present manager, Ben Brown, said those first rural carriers had to carry mail to every house as far out in the country as people lived. Out Navarre Avenue there were houses half way to Cedar Point.

Early mail carriers, crossing orchards and farms between widely spread residences, had to contend with impassable snowdrifts and deep mud (in addition to various animals) as they went about their appointed rounds. Sometimes two men were needed. In bad weather, Mr. Kirk, the station clerk, would drive the horse and buggy of the first rural carrier, Alfred Householder, a Civil War veteran. Together, they could push through mud or shovel through the deep snowbanks they encountered.

Nearly fifty years ago, George Pearson highlighted the career of Eugene N. Davis, the oldest rural carrier in Toledo. Born in 1883, Mr. Davis became a letter carrier at Station A on June 1, 1917.

He recalled clearly the days of driving the rural routes in a horse and buggy. One time, during the severe influenza epidemic of 1917, Mr. Davis' wife drove the route for several months in his absence. By the time of his retirement, he was the vice-president of the National Association of Rural Mail Carriers.

When Mr. Eppstein returned to the main post office, then at St. Clair and Madison, John Quaife became superintendent of Station A. He was followed by Mr. Kirk and then Frank Stransky. After Mr. Stransky died in 1934, John W. Books was appointed superintendent and served for many years. The present superintendent is Michael Seery III. In the early days, clerks and office personel often had to help as substitute carriers whenever a regular carrier failed to show up in the morning.

With the population growing rapidly on the East Side, the postal substation had to expand into new office space. The station moved to 617 Second Street in 1925 (now the VFW Post) and then across the street to larger quarters in the mid 1950s. By the 1940s the original staff of eight had grown to 49 employees. There were nine office workers including the superintendent, 31 regular carriers and three substitutes, as well as three parcel post carriers and three rural carriers in 1944.

Russ Allan recalls working as a substitute carrier in the 1940s and 50s. The pay was 69 cents an hour, and the carrier had to buy his own uniform and insurance. The top salary, after 28 years, was $4100 a year. But the work was steady, and there was always overtime pay at Christmas when carriers would often sort and case mail until 10 or 11 o'clock at night.

Supervisors would sometimes test the honesty of mail carriers by putting money in the mailboxes to see if carriers would take it. One time, Mr. Allan

recalls, a bunch of change was left in a mailbox at
Starr and Main. Knowing it was placed there by a
supervisor, he scattered the coins on the sidewalk
for the kids to have. When he returned to the
station, he was asked if anything unusual had
happened on his route. Mr. Allan replied, "No, and
the coins are not in my pocket either."

Mail delivery on the East Side has come a long
way since the 1850s when Elijah Woodruff, the first
postmaster, used to bring the mail across the river
in a rowboat. Today, Station A is approaching a
century of service, bringing both good news and
bad to the mailboxes of East Toledoans. The first
substation in Toledo, Station A, can be proud of its
long history of delivering the mail.

THE HISTORY OF THE EAST SIDE HOSPITAL

In the first years of the 20th century, a time
when doctors made house calls and most people were
born and died in their own homes, East Toledo did
not have a hospital. Not until 1908 did a young
doctor from Warren, Pennsylvania, begin the East
Side Hospital in his offices in a home on Oak Street.

Dr. Clarence S. Ordway had come to Ohio at
the age of four. His mother had attended school in
Niles, and was a pupil of the later to be President,
William McKinley. The family settled in Bowling
Green, and after graduating from high school there,
young Ordway attended Defiance College, Ohio
Northern, and the University of Maryland where he
received his medical degree. He worked for a while
as the house surgeon at General Hospital in
Baltimore. In 1904 he came to Toledo and was
associated with the Toledo City Hospital, then on
Cherry Street.

While working at Toledo Hospital, Dr. Ordway opened an office in partnership with Dr. Joseph Ely in a house at 1153 Oak Street, near the corner of Fassett. He soon realized the need for a hospital on the East Side to treat emergency and injury cases. Although begun in 1908, the seven-bed hospital did not admit its first patient, East Side photographer Charles Mensing, until February 1910.

From that point, the hospital grew rapidly, adding sixteen more beds in September. A nursing school was added in 1911 when the building was expanded. By the 1940s, up to sixty patients could be treated at the hospital. There were times when more traffic and industrial injuries were treated at the East Side Hospital than at any other hospital in the city. Also, a clinic was established in the early 1930s in the Professional Building that still stands on Starr Avenue at the corner of Garfield Place, and the name "Ordway" can still be seen engraved in the stone over the doorways.

Many people remember having been patients at the East Side Hospital. A postcard dated July 11, 1921, owned by Ted Spillane, records his six-month stay at the hospital for an arm injury sustained trying to rescue a woman from an elevator shaft. Frank Kralik also remembers having his tonsils removed there in July 1946. His stay at the hospital for three days and two nights cost him a total of $28.00.

Dr. Ordway continued as chief surgeon and administrator until 1941, assisted by Dr. Noble and later by Dr. Hemphill. In spite of his busy schedule, Dr. Ordway was a man of many interests. Besides the important offices he held in the Toledo Medical Association, he was also a member of the Chamber of Commerce, the East Toledo Club, the Masons, the Elks, and the O-Ton-Ta-La Grotto. He became fascinated with the motion picture industry during its formative years and collected a large number of

East Side Hospital, 1153 Oak St., Toledo, Ohio.

Postcard view of East Side Hospital.

early and unusual films. He was a friend of William Hart, the western movie idol, and had been invited to visit the famous Hart Ranch.

Dr. Ordway was also an avid hunter and lover of horses and pedigree dogs. In his later years, he purchased and remodeled the old Pioneer Inn on River Road near Grand Rapids, Ohio, which was then over a hundred years old. He continued to live there until his death in 1945 at the age of 71.

Under Dr. Ordway's leadership, the East Side Hospital was known for its excellent care. It had the newest X-ray equipment and its operating room was one of the best in the city. The Blade reported that "some of the outstanding surgical operations of the city have been performed in this modest hospital in Oak Street." A successful appendectomy was performed on a child only a few months old, a difficult operation in the 1930s, and Dr. Ordway was also one of the first surgeons in Toledo to develop spinal anesthesia.

New technology and the expanded need for health care finally outgrew what was possible at such a facility, basically still only an enlarged home. With the opening of St. Charles in the early 1950s, the East Side Hospital was closed. The site (where the Fassett homestead of the 1830s once stood) now became a vacant lot. But the memories remain for many Toledoans who were born or received medical care at the East Side's first hospital in the modest house on Oak Street.

THE EAST SIDE POLICE STATION

Police stations once were located in the neighborhoods they served, and for sixty years the East Side Police Station protected the citizens and was a center for community activities east of the river.

The first East Side station was established about the turn of the century in the former No. 6 Engine House at First and Euclid. The fire station, which had been in the building for many years, moved to its new location at Main and Starr Avenue about 1895.

Captain W. A. Williams, chief of detectives, became the first officer in command of the East Side station. At that time, the station had one patrol wagon, and the policemen covered not only the East Side but also the district north of Cherry Street to parts of the West End.

In the years just prior to World War I, Captain Jonas (Dick) Hadley was in charge of the East Side district. He was a Civil War veteran who had served under General Phil Sheridan, the famous Union cavalry leader. According to George Pearson, Captain Hadley once had a clock at the station that wouldn't run. One day, a pail of water was boiling on the old oak stove, and Capt. Hadley threw the clock in the water and left it for several hours. When he finally pulled it out, all the grease and oil that had clogged the works had boiled away and the clock kept perfect time.

Lieutenant Frank Reilly was the next to be in command of the station. He was in charge when an officer was sent to settle a dispute over a horse who had destroyed a neighbor's corn and vegetables. The angry neighbor had penned the animal in a chicken house and would not let it out. When the policeman reported that he had freed the horse, Lieutenant Reilly replied, "I hope you didn't break the lock." To that the officer responded, "No, I just tore the hinges off the door."

Among the other policemen during those early days were Sergeants William Rudd and William Watson, Lieutenant Fred Stonehouse who always preferred the night shift, Detective Ed Rock, and Capt. D. M. O'Sullivan. Capt. O'Sullivan was an old veteran of the force who was one of the first desk officers at the East Side station until he retired in 1914 at the age of 68. He liked to recall adventures from earlier in his career.

Once Capt. O'Sullivan was assigned to guard an excursion train to Niagara Falls, on which pickpockets had been victimizing wealthy travelers. After leaving the jurisdiction of Toledo, the robbers became bold. Catching the thieves in the act, the policemen took matters into their own hands and forced the pickpockets to jump off the rear of the moving train. In spite of such incidents, Capt. O'Sullivan was remembered as a kind-hearted gentleman who always tried to help the poor and unfortunate.

Capt. William Schultz succeeded Lieut. Reilly, and was in charge when the station moved to its new building at Second and Oswald Streets in 1925. This larger police headquarters also housed the city traffic engineer and the police academy for the city's Civil Defense. In addition, by 1942 a dental clinic had offices in the building, as did Mr. Pearson of The Blade.

By the late 1950's, maintaining the East Side station was called "a waste of manpower" and it was decided to centralize police headquarters downtown. The building was sold in 1959 to the Boys' Club of Toledo for $75,000 and is still in use today. The old police station was once an important part of the community that many East Siders can remember visiting, most of whom had not broken any laws.

First Police Station at First & Main, c. 1900.

"THE SUN" ENLIGHTENED THE EAST SIDE FOR 64 YEARS

On November 5, 1920, the first issue of "The East Side Sun" was published, and the weekly paper owned and edited by the Toppin family continued to appear in East Toledo homes until April 3rd, 1984. During its 64-year history, The Sun kept Toledoans east of the river informed about local events, church news, and stories that were important for the whole city.

James Toppin, who was born in Toronto, Canada, learned the newspaper trade as a copy boy on the Cincinnati Enquirer and as a printer with the Cincinnati Post. After working for other papers in Dayton and Hamilton, Mr. Toppin went to New York City and got a job on the New York Sun. Soon, however, he decided he wanted to have his own paper and came back to Ohio in 1919 and bought the Genoa Times. He ran that paper for a year before moving to the fast-growing area of East Toledo.

Mr. Toppin, whose motto was "Pay your bills and tell the truth," was fortunate to have the help of his wife Isabel Whitehouse Toppin, an accomplished writer and poet. She not only helped write news stories, but also solicited ads, kept books, and managed the front office. "For many years," Mr. Toppin recalled, "it was an uphill fight." Often he was in the office all night, dropping on a couch for a few hours rest before resuming his work.

An experienced linotype operator, Mr. Toppin

had the ability to "set type" for his stories from just a few notes. This gave him an advantage over other editors who had to first compose their articles on a typewriter. During his year in Genoa when the town was struck by a tornado, Mr. Toppin was able to set up the whole five-column front page story from memory.

Many of James and Isabel Toppin's concerns about Toledo are still relevant today. In a February 1944 article, Mr. Toppin spoke of the "enormous saving to the taxpayer" by the "consolidation of city and county governments," eliminating the need for "two sets of officials working on the same job." He was also "a strong advocate" for building a bridge "from Ironville to Manhattan" at a time when such a river crossing could have been accomplished much quicker and at far less cost. In addition, Mr. Toppin believed property owners bore too much of the tax burden, which discouraged people from building new homes.

Always strong boosters of the East Side, the Toppins proudly promoted the area's schools, businesses, parks, and churches, a tradition which was carried on by the second generation of the family. James Toppin died in 1949, two years after his son Paul had joined the business. Isabel Toppin continued as Editor-in-Chief for several years before her death in 1968, but much of the work had already passed to Paul and his wife Doris.

Paul Toppin had graduated from Waite and attended the University of Cincinnati and the University of Toledo. He served in the U.S. Navy during World War II, and later worked as a machinist at Wright Field in Dayton before joining his parents' paper.

The East Side Sun had begun publishing in a rented office at 504 Main Street, and then moved to 230 Main a few years later. On September 22, 1926, ground was broken for the building at 512 Fourth Street where the offices remained for nearly 60 more years. The cost of a subscription in 1923 was only $1.50 a year. But in December 1925, it was decided to increase circulation by offering the paper on a free basis as an incentive to advertisers, and ten thousand copies were distributed. By 1970, there were 18,500 copies being printed every week.

Paul and Doris Toppin continued to edit and publish The Sun until its closing in 1984. Other long-time employees who helped with the paper over the years were Clarence Loeb, Ruth Kleine, Doris Jones, Agnes Harris, Shirley Gladieux, Joe Ehret, and many more.

The Toppins are still active in the community and members of the East Toledo Historical Society, to which they donated back issues of the paper. East Siders can be grateful to the Toppin family for not only promoting the events of the community, but also for preserving a record of the important moments in peoples' lives over a period of nearly 64 years.

HISTORY OF LOCKE BRANCH LIBRARY

Last year Locke Branch Library at Main Street and Greenwood celebrated its 75th anniversary serving residents of East Toledo. It is a Carnegie library, one of the earliest branch libraries in the city, opening its doors for the first time on December 5, 1917.

Between 1886 and 1919 Andrew Carnegie, the industrialist who started the mammoth United States Steel Corporation in Pittsburgh, donated more than $40 million for the building of 1,679 public libraries in cities all around the country. Many of his libraries have since been closed or replaced by newer buildings, but Locke Branch remains as one of the few Carnegie libraries left in Toledo.

As early as 1905, Carnegie offered Toledo $100,000 for the construction of branch libraries, but for some reason the gift was not accepted at that time. By 1911 plans were being made to build a library on the site of Waite High School adjacent to where the new school was then being erected. The city, however, could not commit the necessary operating funds and the library was not built. Then in 1916 Carnegie increased his donation to $125,000 to build five branch libraries in Toledo, and the offer was accepted.

The East Side branch was named for David Ross Locke (1833–1888), former editor of The Blade who wrote the popular Petroleum V. Nasby letters that were published throughout the nation. Nasby, a satiric figure Locke used to promote his anti-slavery views, was a favorite of President Lincoln. Not many East Siders know that Valleywood was once named Nasby Street.

Mr. Locke also published speeches by Morrison R. Waite as early as 1865, and helped bring national exposure to the Maumee lawyer who became Chief Justice of the Supreme Court. Mr. Locke's son, Robinson Locke, helped dedicate the new East Side library by donating the large portrait of his father which is still prominently displayed.

The day Locke Branch opened in 1917, only 188 books were placed in circulation. By the end of the first year of operation, however, 90,244 books had been borrowed. In 1919, magazines were added to the collection. During the Depression year of 1932, circulation reached a new high of 201,034 items borrowed by the public.

The first librarian at Locke Branch was Emma Crowell, and she was followed by Helen Welker. Over the years, circulating libraries were located for a time at Oakdale and Navarre Schools, and of course another branch was built in Birmingham that still continues to serve the community.

In late 1935, Locke Branch was enlarged 75% by adding a new reading area to the front of the building, increasing the office space, rearranging the stairwells, and adding more space to the basement meeting room. Mary Kessler was head librarian at the time of the remodeling. Also at this time, a rustic Lincoln log cabin made by J. G. Fair of the West Toledo library found a home at Locke Branch.

Two other important gifts originally given to the East Side library are now downtown in the Local History Department of the main library. One is the Machen portrait of Peter Navarre. The other gift was the huge volume of the history of the Ford Post, G.A.R., containing Capt. George Scheets' hand-written accounts of every East Sider who fought during the Civil War.

Over the years, Locke Branch has continued to receive modern changes. In 1962, it was closed from July 28th to November 5th for another remodeling. Ceilings were lowered, new lighting and carpeting was installed, and some of the old windows were improved. Also, to the dismay of some patrons, the children's room was redone by replacing the dark wood fireplace with more shelving.

Land for a rear parking lot was purchased in 1979. During the 1980's new wiring, carpeting, and air-conditioning were installed, and audio and video-cassettes were added to the library's collection. The circulation desk was computerized in 1986, and in 1990 the card catalogue also went on line. More items are borrowed today than ever before, and now

over 75 years old, Locke Branch continues to be an
important part of the East Side community.

END OF THE STREETCAR ERA IN EAST TOLEDO

Over a hundred years ago, in 1892, the first
electric streetcars began running in East Toledo
when a line crossed the Cherry Street Bridge and
ran out Front Street to Millard Avenue in Ironville.
Soon three other lines were added: the Oak Street,
East Broadway, and Starr Avenue.   The Starr
Avenue line was the last to serve the East Side,
making its final run on July 7, 1939.

During the heyday of the electric streetcars
in the early 1900s, Toledo had 17 lines with a fleet
of at least 225 trolleys that ran on 120 miles of track
over 69 miles of streets and carried some 50 million
passengers a year.   But by the 1920s, automobiles
and more mobile buses began replacing the old
trolleys.   The last electric streetcar in Toledo ran
on the Long Belt line in 1949.

Before there were electric streetcars, horse-
drawn trolleys slogged along the city's often muddy
streets.   George Parks, an early East Side funeral
director, remembered the heavy pull upgrade on
Main Street for the poor trolley-horses.   Also,
occasionally the cars would "bounce off the rails and
it was no little job getting them back again."   The
first trolley barn on the East Side had a large turn-
table for turning the cars around and was located at
Starr and Main before Engine House #6 was built
there in 1895.

The Community Traction Company operated the
four East Toledo lines.   The Front Street line ran
out Front to Ironville.   The Oak Street line followed

Oak to Fassett and then out Miami to the Rossford limits. The other two lines ran along Main and Starr with the East Broadway line following that street out to the turn-around at Vinal and the Starr Avenue line continuing out Starr to the Dearborn turn-around. All the lines crossed the Cherry Street Bridge and proceeded through the downtown to various parts of the city.

Originally, all the lines were single-track with switches one-quarter or one-half miles apart. This led to many delays on the crowded streets, and in time all the lines were double-tracked with the exception of the Starr Avenue line.

From the 1890s until 1930 the car barn for the electric trolleys was located on Starr Avenue at Valleywood where the Sports Center is today. It had repair shops and cleaning facilities, and was also where the motormen and conductors assembled each day. Many businesses and restaurants soon opened in the area, such as Stoiber's 3-cent lunch room across the street.

The Front Street line was the first to close in 1926 when the street was repaved. The Oak Street line was abandoned in the mid-1930s, and the East Broadway line closed a few years later when that street was also repaved, leaving only the Starr Avenue line still operating. The large trolley barn had closed in 1930 when all the cars were moved to the Central Avenue headquarters.

A large ceremony was held in 1939 when the last streetcar on the Starr Avenue line made its final run. Seventy-five East Toledo civic leaders, city officials, and Community Traction executives rode in the big yellow car as it "rumbled, swayed, and lurched over the Starr avenue tracks for the last time." Speeches were delivered by Mayor Roy Start, Frank Wiley of the East Toledo Club, and Fred J. Young who was the chairman of the festivities.

With Mr. Young at the controls, the streetcar led a parade of six new buses loaded with over 100 prominent East Siders. Crowds lined Main Street shouting greetings and snapping pictures as the trolley went by. Inside the car, the occupants "sang lustily to the accompaniment of two accordians."

As luck would have it, the Cherry Street Bridge was up when the procession reached that point. During the delay, Mr. John Ehrle, who later became a well-known entertainer and opera singer, delivered two rousing numbers. After making the downtown loop, the passengers transferred to the new buses and returned following the same route. The streetcar era had ended for East Toledo.

Car 301, Ironville, at Front & Millard.

THE EAST SHALL RISE AGAIN

The headline read: "East Toledo Civic Association Asks City Secession Ruling." The article stated that taxpayers east of the river felt they were not receiving their fair share of city services. But the date on the newspaper was not 1993. It was April 20, 1937.

At the meeting, a resolution was adopted to ask the Attorney General of Ohio for an opinion on the legality of the East Side seceding from the city of Toledo. Members of the Civic Association denied that the motion, which was introduced by Birmingham businessman Paul Juhasz, was intended as "a threat." It passed, however, by an almost unanimous vote.

The complaints of 54 years ago all have a familiar sound. The city had delayed work on the Wheeling Street sewer project, and some felt that a secession vote could exert political pressure to get the job done. Others were dissatisfied with a nine-member Council that was not representative of voters in some parts of the city.

Among those who first advocated leaving the city was William "Brig" Young. He said that "an independent city on the East Side of the river had been his hope for years." Another secessionist was William Rundell, who administered a sales tax agency but lost his license when Democrats took control of county government.

Strong talk of secession was also heard during the 1950's when the city of Oregon was incorporated as a separate municipality. It is interesting to speculate how development would have been different if the East Side and Oregon were one community.

Of course, nothing has come from all the talk, and a local civil war has never happened. But the grievances are still heard. Low-income housing projects have been added and the East Side Police Station was taken away. The B & O railroad bridge at Fassett and Stillman has been closed to traffic and slowly rotting for years. Streets are not plowed in winter or repaired in summer, and there is still at this writing no representative from East Toledo on the nine-member City Council.

Even in the early days, the East Side was not wanted by Toledo. It did not become the 6th Ward of the city until the 1850s, and only then because the major railroad lines terminated east of the river. The city was also hesitant to build a bridge, fearing competition from the East Side, and for many years a prohibitive toll had to be paid every time the river was crossed. And the East Side riverfront, occupied by heavy industry for most of its history, now has been largely neglected even though much of it is a beautiful park.

But all in all, it is probably fortunate the East Side remains part of the city. The historic river corridor is preserved. The possibilities for development survive. Hopefully, without a single cannon being fired, the East shall rise again. Not as an independent city, but as a part of a rejuvenated and appreciative city of Toledo.

About the Author

Larry Michaels grew up in East Toledo, living at 439 Arden Place until he was seven, and then moving to 821 Butler and later to 852 Butler (the house his mother grew up in) shortly before leaving for college. He attended Franklin and Navarre elementary schools and graduated from Waite. He was a member of St. Mark Lutheran Church, and he also frequented every tennis court in East Toledo.

Since returning to Toledo ten years ago as Resource Pastor of Hope Lutheran Church, he has become active in the East Toledo Historical Society and has been amazed to discover the rich heritage of the well-preserved but generally unappreciated neighborhoods east of the river. This book has grown out of those discoveries. He and his wife Suzi own the Bihl House at St. Louis & Greenwood, where the Historical Society maintains a library for East Side research.

Author at Waite's 75th Anniversary, 1989.

Index